on

Between Decoustruction and New Modernism

Jean Nouvel

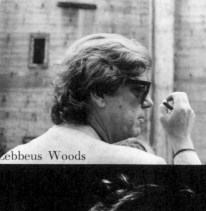

Lebbeus Woods

Bernard Tschumi

Michael Sorkin

Zaha Hadid

Peter Eisenman

Daniel Libeskind

Wolf D. Prix
(Coop Himmelblau)

Helmut Swiczinsky

Thom Mayne (Morphos

Architecture in Transition

Between Deconstruction
and New Modernism

Edited by Peter Noever
MAK — Austrian Museum of Applied Arts, Vienna
Assisted by Regina Haslinger

Introduction by Alois Martin Müller.
Contributions by

Coop Himmelblau
Peter Eisenman
Zaha Hadid
Daniel Libeskind
Morphosis
Jean Nouvel
Michael Sorkin
Bernard Tschumi and
Lebbeus Woods.

Epilogue by Philip Johnson

Prestel

Photograph Credits, see page 159

Front cover: Coop Himmelblau,
"Jasmac Bar Building,"
Saporro, Japan. 1989

Translations by Eileen Martin and Abigail Ryan

Prestel-Verlag, Mandlstraße 26, D-8000 Munich 40, Germany
Tel: (89) 38 17 09 0; Fax: (89) 38 17 09 35

Distributed in continental Europe by Prestel-Verlag Verlegerdienst München GmbH & Co KG
Gutenbergstraße 1, D-8031 Gilching, Germany
Tel: (8105) 21 10; Fax: (8105) 55 20

Distributed in the USA and Canada by te Neues Publishing Company,
15 East 76th Street, New York, NY 10021, USA
Tel: (212) 288 0265; Fax: (212) 570 2373

Distributed in Japan by YOHAN-Western Publications Distribution Agency, 14 – 9 Okubo 3-chome,
Shinjuku-ku, J-Tokyo 169
Tel: (3) 208 0181; Fax: (3) 209 0288

Distributed in the United Kingdom, Ireland and all remaining countries by Thames & Hudson
Limited, 30 – 40 Bloomsbury Street, London WC1B 3 QP, England
Tel: (71) 636 5488; Fax: (71) 636 4799

Color separations by Karl Dörfel-Repro GmbH, Munich
Typeset, printed and bound by Bosch-Druck, Landshut/Ergolding
Printed in Germany

ISBN 3-7913-1136-0 (English edition)
ISBN 3-7913-1116-6 (German edition)

Contents

Peter Noever

ON ARCHITECTURE TODAY

Perhaps it is a rebellion of feelings which, off the main path of a linear architectural development and undeterred by shattered utopias, is providing a possible start for a new and visionary architectural language as the end of the century approaches. A certain strategic development is becoming evident. At the points of friction between Modernism, Postmodernism, Postavant-garde and Poststructuralism an idea is emerging which historiography, falling over itself to be ahead of the times, is trying to package and sell as Deconstructivism, as a new architectural fashion, even as an extension of the Constructivist movement of the twenties. Historiography knows but ignores the fact that the Constructivist framework, with its new way of seeing, its transformed Weltanschauung, had already based itself in the final analysis on a Deconstructivist idea, an idea regarding art and architecture that separates, severs, breaks, fragments, but that at the same time, has reconstituted the bits and pieces gained in the process into a comprehensive principle, causing them to become the essential characteristic of modern twentieth-century art.

So it seemed not only an intriguing but also a necessary task to face up to the challenge of the moment and put on a series of lectures by those artists who through their work play a decisive part in the architectural discussion of today: Morphosis, Daniel Libeskind, Zaha Hadid, Jean Nouvel, Peter Eisenman, Lebbeus Woods, Michael Sorkin, Bernard Tschumi, Coop Himmelblau. What actually links them, what do they have in common? Is their affinity only confined, perhaps, to the demontage of all those fundamental principles of architecture that were valid in the past, the rejection of all traditions and the principle of perfection — although without generating new utopias, as the modern movement has done?

Architecture then — architecture now? Up until the present day there has not been a convincing explanation of the significance of the stone construction in Gizeh: it remains an enigma. A magical sign of a magical system of thought?

7

Is the loss of theory as the basis of a potentially thriving architecture thus prolonged? Does theory therefore still continue to follow practice? Architecture which is understood as architecture never allows a one-sided interpretation. Universal character is the real criterion of architecture.

Architecture now — architecture then. Its claim to be apprehended as a metaphor of space, time and corporeality and yet remain enigmatic has not been changed. The same applies to the most convincing form of elementary architecture, the pyramid of Cheops. This mighty structure, presumably concealing an indecipherable code, an archaic monument in the guise of a tomb, simultaneously expresses both enlightenment and aversion, a powerful symbol of the life and of the spirit and the return of human existence to the earth. Since then theory and practice have moved inexorably away from each other and have never recovered their unity.

The actual, direct confrontation with the architect and his work, is now more of an imperative challenge than ever, at least when it has to do with an evaluation of architecture free from categorizations and pigeon-holing, according to its actual essence, its autonomous program. These were more or less the considerations that led to the series of lectures "Architecture Today" at the MAK (Austrian Museum for Applied Art).

Whatever their differences and sometimes outright opposition in points of view and origins, the architects presented here are nevertheless the expression of an age, of a critical attitude towards our technology and technology of thought, of an attack on a society that is homogeneous and yet devoid of inner substance.

Alois Martin Müller

THE DIALECTIC OF MODERNISM

More than twenty years ago a philosopher in Paris began looking into the all-too logical constructions of the modern world. In recent years Jacques Derrida's ideas have come to play an important part in architectural discussion, and this is due to a growing awareness of the problem-situations and aporias into which a dialectic of enlightenment has brought our civilization.

According to Theodor W. Adorno and Max Horkheimer[1], the "dialectic of enlightenment" means: in order to become an autonomous subject, man has to distance himself from nature and the dark primeval forces. This necessary process of distantiation helps man to learn increasingly to control himself and nature. This liberation from diffuse dependencies − and this is the origin of subjectivity − now becomes hybrid and turns against man himself: he falls prey to his natural need to dominate, and the dominator of nature becomes the prey of nature. On this centrifugal flight-path away from the origin man again entangles himself at every step in the mythical dependence he originally wanted to escape, that is, the mythology of the dominance of the world and of man through a force of reason that is now only instrumental, applied exclusively to domination. The sociologist Max Weber, albeit not acknowledging its culturally negative substrate, has described this process as the great rationalization process of the Western world.

In the fine arts, this process is reflected most effectively in architecture. This is understandable, because, as an art that functions in the world we live in and has to prove itself and serve a purpose, architecture is most closely bound up with scientific and technical rationality. The extent of rationalization and functionalization is however not prescribed by any objective values. In the first three decades of the twentieth century many architects consciously adapted their work to the process of social rationalization, because they wanted it to express the rational advance of mankind.

---

[1] Horkheimer, Max and Adorno, Theodor W.:
Dialektik der Aufklärung: Philosophische Fragmente.
S. Fischer, Frankfurt/M. 1969.

Alongside the dialectic of enlightenment there is also a dialectic of modernism. Parallel, as it were, to the triumphal progress of instrumental reason runs a movement that mistrusts this reason, criticizes it, and unmasks its mythical character. The dialectic of modernism means that the exclusively rational construction of logic, progress, totality, etc., is opposed by a movement that sees through these constructions as such. This movement deconstructs these constructions. The two movements impinge on each other at best as correctives and, to borrow a term from Heraclitus, they maintain a kind of antagonistic rapport.

All the articles by architects in this volume aim to stir up a modernism that has become all too quiet and static and to break open fundamentals and fundamentalisms with architectural methods. These architects have subjected their métier to the same kind of examination as Derrida applied to textual matter. So I shall briefly outline Derrida's basic ideas, not — I must expressly state — in an attempt to stick yet another uniform label on the architects assembled here and suggest false connections and proximities, but because the romantic idea of the "mutual illumination of the arts" is still a useful aid to understanding interrelations.

What Derrida calls "deconstruction" is not a comprehensive theory, nor is it a systematic fabric of ideas. Deconstruction is a strategy, a way of reading philosophical or literary texts in order to get to the bottom of them. The following questions need to be answered: What do authors do to be able to postulate unassailable truths and absolute concepts in their works? What do they do to convincingly justify and assert the basic principles or foundations on which their theories are based? And failing this: to what lengths will they go, what subterfuges and simplifications are they prepared to employ, in order to arrive at a philosophy that fully accords with their view of reality? Deconstruction means burrowing deep, to find out what unconscious premises a text is based on and what the blind spot in the author's eye cannot see. Man seems to have the fatal ability to build up a philosophical apparatus to which he subordinates and adapts reality through a kind of pre-established harmony; thus reality is fitted into a philosophical system. Derrida, then, analyzes texts via philosophical interrogation. First, the conceptual hierarchies immanent in the systems of thought have to be clarified, because "in a classical antithesis we are faced not with the philosophical coexistence of a vis-à-vis but with a powerful hierarchy"[2]. In our work of excavation we have to find out how the hierarchies evolve, how they explain and legitimize themselves.

Deconstruction is not at all a superior kind of reason, for then it would have had to build up a system that could prove its superiority. This

[2] Derrida, Jacques: *Positionen.* Edition Passagen, Graz 1986, p. 88.

would bring us back to the carrousel of oppositions and thinking in a "true/false" schematism, that is, we would be back to hierarchical thinking. Deconstruction does not attack the existing structures from outside, it can only achieve something if it resides within the system: "Deconstruction necessarily has to operate from inside, to make use of all the subversive, strategic and economic tools of the old structure, that is, it is not allowed to remove particular atoms and elements therefrom"[3]. So the program reads: overturn, work from inside, break open. We might go so far as to say that a kind of virus is fed into a system and then spooks around inside it, working not to destroy the program but to reveal the conceptual structure, the pyramid of concepts: to fathom the unconscious drives, find the blind spot, which can only be seen from outside.

The basic principles on which these structures are based are always of a metaphysical nature, says Derrida. "Metaphysics" is what Aristotle called the philosophy that he discussed "after physics" in his writings, and which dealt with things "beyond physics," like essence, existence, substance, etc. This meta-world isolates the phenomena and regards them as unchanging, as always there and always in order. Derrida now shows in his analyses that all names for reasoning, principle or center are metaphysical concepts, which emerge like erratic blocks from the mists of history. At the same time, all metaphysical concepts are "invariants of a presence."[4] The directness of the received impression, the assertion of final truths for a divine consciousness, the assumption of an origin for history, the spontaneous, unmediated intuition, the truth behind physical appearances — all these ideas are based on insights that are seemingly evident. Precisely the modern cultural scene with its cult of the new, with its upvaluation of the transitory, the fleeting and the ephemeral, has a great affinity with the idea of the metaphysical presence.

The metaphysical concepts are the foundations for whole systems of thought, which they justify and hierarchize. In doing so they also hierarchize the world of ideas and of life. This means, for instance, that in pairs of antitheses, that expression which has the greatest proximity to the immediate presence, to immediacy, is always accorded greater importance in human thought. Because hierarchization is always active, the quest for basic principles or for a centered structure becomes a particular journey: a journey in search of immediacy, origin, pure receptivity, unity. This quest for the grail becomes in Derrida's formulation "the undertaking of a 'strategic' return, in the form of an idealization, to an origin or a priority that is seen as simple, intact, normal, pure, exemplary, self-identical, so that from this premise the derivation, the complication, the decay, the chance, etc., can be considered. All

[3] Derrida, Jacques: *Grammatologie.* Suhrkamp, Frankfurt/M. 1983 p. 45.

[4] Derrida, Jacques: "Die Struktur, das Zeichen und das Spiel im Diskurs der Wissenschaften vom Menschen." In: *Die Schrift und die Differenz.* Suhrkamp, Frankfurt/M. 1972, p. 424.

metaphysicists, from Plato to Rousseau, from Descartes to Husserl, have proceeded in this way: the good before the bad, the positive before the negative, the pure before the impure, the essential before the chance . . . . It is *the* metaphysical precepts, altogether the most constant, deepest and strongest procedure."[5]

[5] Derrida, Jacques: *Limited Inc.* Supplement to *Glyph* 2, Baltimore 1977, p. 236.

In Modernist architecture the rationality of the exact sciences and origin-centered thinking go hand in hand. The modernization processes call into question all truths all of the time, so that comprehensive meaning or sense is fragmented into ever smaller sense-particles. This fragmentation makes the holistic vision ever harder to uphold, but many artists and architects refuse to accept the situation, attempting to reconstruct from the fragments of the disintegrating world a whole, true, and essential world-view. The pure geometrical forms seem to express these true and essential substrates best. They are the physical embodiment, the *sermo corporeus* of that which the terms for immediacy, first cause and center conceptually express for the metaphysicists. In order to be essential and true, the forms have to be formally simple, intact, normal, pure, exemplary and irreducible, without rhetorical ornamentation. The form itself is thus given a metaphysical charge, the pure elementary figures become metaphysical figures. So here, too, we have a strategic return in the form of an idealization — towards unity and simplicity, first cause and origin. This is the myth of origin of classical Modernism as represented by functionalism and rationalism.

All the architects who spoke to us in Vienna are concerned with new architectural thinking. They are working to disencumber architecture of too limited a scientific, technical rationality — and of the symbols of such a rationality — with the aid of reason. They are aware of the dangers of reason-become-mythic, and so they allow greater skepticism regarding reason. They are no longer seekers for paradise, nor are they progressive "back-to-the-origins" regressives, they are strategists against overhasty harmonization. Their way of thinking no longer proceeds from an ideality, an essence, or a true nature as a basis for architecture. They are anti-fundamentalists without being groundless, and — because they have suspended metaphysics — they are involved in a process of shifting.

Bernard Tschumi has long been concerned with the theme of transgression in relation to architecture: with pleasure and violence, with eros and decay, with madness and chance, with fields that go beyond the limits of a discursive reason. For a long time his theoretical endeavors were devoted to the "other" side of architecture, the repressed, the taboo, the banished sensual element that disrupts or even destroys forms. There have been few attempts in architecture to exploit the poetry of chance, irony as radical criticism, stylistic incongruity, or the technique of collage and montage. Decentralization, disjunction, juxtaposition, heterogeneity and fragmentation are thus the cornerstones of Tschumi's architectural approach.

Peter Eisenman is concerned with the loss of the central position, the growing eccentricity of man in the modern age. For architecture, this means that there is no longer anything it can relate to: neither to man as the measure of all things nor to such self-created fictions as reason and history. Eisenman is the cultural and psychoanalytical "shift"-worker among architects; he puts architecture on the couch, so to speak, and decomposes and demystifies the gospels of historical philosophy and reason which architecture embraced and unquestioningly accepted. Eisenman has seen through the illusion of linking rationality with truth and transparency and classical Modernism's illusion of eternity.

The project for the extension to the Berlin Museum incorporating a Jewish Museum would necessarily have confronted any architect with the problem of the "dialectic of enlightenment". Daniel Libeskind's project is not based on a beginning, it has no center, and the walls tilt. The Museum cannot of course be the expression of a historical construction in the Hegelian sense, linking the philosophy of enlightenment and history, and consequently assuming that the historical process is based on a reasonable principle. In our century totalitarianisms have radically destroyed Hegel's historical optimism. Libeskind's design is a metaphor for a historical catastrophe. It tells of historical crimes, whose declared aim was genocide, and whose traces may well be lost because the extermination actually took place and has left a huge, ineradicable vacuum.

To develop subversive force against the power-hungriness of a merely restrictive rationality and architectural functionality is not just the privilege of theory. There is something much more tangible that rebels against suffocation and uniformity: the body, the feeling. The "open architecture" of Coop Himmelblau, a team consisting of Wolf D. Prix and Helmut Swiczinsky, refuses to kowtow to the dictates of the feasible, to practical constraints; their designs are born of body-language, of dynamic gesture. With as little control as possible the feeling for a building is "thrown" onto paper, so that the passion and the directness, the energy and the enthusiasm are retained. Their fractured architecture produces precisely that sort of jarring which others normally try to eliminate. By giving free rein to a repertoire of gestures — tilting, twisting, piercing, breaching, slitting — they create through confrontation an architecture of lucid, poetic spaces contrasted with "leftover" spaces. Each in their own way, Michael Sorkin, Zaha M. Hadid and Morphosis oppose the official "styles of reason," as Sorkin calls them; they oppose the tyranny of the Cartesian system and a minimalism that pretends to depth and numinosity. Instead of repeating under ever new guises what has already been verified, a fallible architecture should be given a chance in a world in which planning is in any case half fictional because of the time-dynamic. After looking into the Suprematism of Kazimir Malevich, Zaha Hadid began to set planes and bodies in motion. When she goes so far as to suspend them in mid-air, it is because after the loss of gravity overlayerings emerge which can be productively utilized for architecture. And the architecture of Morphosis — Thom Mayne and Michael Rotondi — reveals the texture of a heterogeneous society. In their hands, building becomes the ability to leave the individual part-systems their autonomy and nevertheless join them together to a whole by not blurring the transitions.

Jean Nouvel believes that there is no longer a prescribed path for the architect of today. Hence he attemptes to infiltrate doubt into his projects, doubt regarding any kind of simplification or official premise. Large buildings, which he often designs, have a curious ambiguity about them: on the one hand there is a tendency toward simplification and clarity, on the other they become ever more complex. Nouvel attempts to resolve this paradox between complexity and simplicity and lightness with associative reasoning, with lateral thinking.

Lebeus Woods is the visionary creator of the total work of art among the architects assembled here. His strangely bent *bricolages* (to be understood in the positive sense of Lévi-Strauss) not only float in the air (in some cases), they also balance precariously between the optimistic metaphysics of the artiste, which seeks to hold or force together again a disintegrated world, and deep skepticism.

The architects presented in this volume are no longer deductive rationalists, no longer interpreters of a uniform philosophy; they are something more complex and also less determinate. They confront us with the paradox and tragedy of our culture, as perceived by the sociologist Georg Simmel: it is a paradox that life flows but has to be conducted through solid forms, that it can only become formed in this way; tragic is a cultural misdirection, in which life becomes less and less capable of assimilating these solid products and becomes alienated from them. Modernism has always known a variety of aggregate conditions; now it is on the march again, to dissolve the crystalline formations without the constraint of uniformity into multistratiformity.

Wolf D. Prix

ON THE EDGE

Not for nothing am I showing you our team photo (see p. 2) right at the beginning of this talk: it is important you should know that my friend Helmut Swiczinsky and I together developed all the Coop Himmelblau projects you will see.

I have just come from our studio in Los Angeles, and each time I arrive in Vienna, I ask myself how the difference between the two cities can be explained. Firstly, Los Angeles has 14 million inhabitants. Secondly, trends are born in Los Angeles that are taken up, if very unwillingly, in New York, and later come over to Europe; I have never heard of a trend moving from Vienna to Los Angeles. Thirdly, there is a fundamental difference in the treatment of architects: in Los Angeles no-one bothers about the architecture or the architects, unlike Vienna, where everyone is an architect and everyone is concerned about architecture (whether that is an advantage is another question).

Of course Vienna has a long tradition, and I am sure you know the story of Siccardsburg and van der Null, who built the Vienna State Opera-House. When the building-work was already in progress, it was decided to raise the Ringstrasse one meter. The architects fought the measure desperately, but to no avail. The Emperor came to the opening and said quite casually to his adjutant: "The building is too low." The adjutant passed the comment on to the press, and the press made it public opinion. The opera-house was held to be out of proportion and too low. The architect read the article, and went home and shot himself. When the Emperor heard of this he was horrified and determined never to express his opinion in public again. So from then on he only said, "It was very nice it has been a pleasure." So much on the treatment of architects in Vienna.

The title of this evening's lecture is "On the Edge," and I am going to talk about designing twisted, tilted and fragmented structures, about open architecture.

---

1. Jasmac Bar Building,
Sapporo, Japan, 1989

What is "open architecture?" Or perhaps it would be better to ask how should we think, plan and build in a world that is becoming daily more and more fragmented? Should we turn a blind eye to this fragmentation and take refuge in an "ideal" world of architecture? As practiced Viennese we know very well that turning a blind eye to something costs an enormous amount of energy and imagination, energy and imagination which should be put into projects; but quite apart from that, there is no ideal world of architecture any more, nor will there ever be again.

Does "open architecture" mean that the architecture, the building, is not complete, or that it is transparent, or has no doors or windows? No, it does not mean any of that. To us, "open architecture" means architecture that is initially not for a specific purpose, self-sufficient structures that form differentiated spaces, spaces that do not pin down the future user but self-sufficiently offer him a range of possibilities. What we originally had in mind were structures like the old commercial buildings that were later converted to other uses. Since 1965 we have been fascinated by these "lofts" — huge empty sheds with no fixed purpose. And so we began to design loft structures. In our imagination these were shell structures that were not dedicated to a particular use.

The Hot Flat project, designed in 1978, was the next step (fig. 2). In this project we were no longer solely concerned with large neutral sheds, but also with elements that differentiate these sheds. In this case it is a community room that shoots through the building like a burning arrow, its flames forming a glass roof which covers the court. This roof of flames cuts through individual apartments and begins to carve out corners and edges — corners and edges that initially do not appear to make any sense, but which permit spatial differentiation.

The flame is a perfect paradigm for mutation of form. Mutations of form have always fascinated us, and they ultimately led us to the idea of the twisted and tilted structures. The arrow-like structure that pushes straight through the building in the Hot Flat project becomes a tilted element in the Merz School project of 1981 (fig. 3). In 1982, in the Residential Housing Vienna 2 project, we went a step further: we twisted and tilted two structures against each other and combined them with a flame (fig. 4). This created spaces inside that are differentiated, like landscapes. They are initially neutral, and are to be completed and utilized by the user later.

This concept was the ideal starting-point for a competition for a youth center in Berlin in 1983 (fig. 5). In this project it seemed meaningful to us to provide spaces the young people could later take possession of and complete. Spaces without a specific purpose, divided up only roughly, but differentiated and interrelated. The sheds should challenge the users to

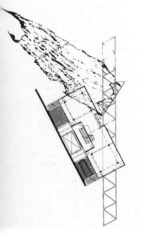

2. Hot Flat,
Vienna, 1978.
Floor plan

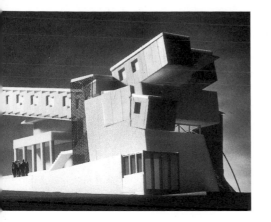

*3. Merzschule,
Stuttgart, 1981.
Model*

*4. Wien 2
residential
complex, Vienna,
1983. Model*

be active. We did not win this competition, and the reason given for rejecting our work was that this concept would make it impossible to administer the youth center. We could hardly imagine a greater compliment.

Now I should like to say something about design itself. The German language is very precise here. The word for design, *Entwurf*, consists of the prefix *Ent-* ("out," "away," "dis-") — as in *entflammen* ("flare up"), *sich entäussern* ("divest oneself") — and the verb *werfen* ("throw"). So it describes the process of designing as a very complex and dynamic act.

In the last five to ten years we have begun to shorten the actual process of design, to condense it. We do discuss the project, but we do not discuss the spatial repercussions. We try to define the feeling, the emotion that the space is later to radiate. And then suddenly we have a drawing, sometimes on a sheet of paper, sometimes on the table,

*5. Youth center,
Berlin, 1983. Model*

sometimes even on the wall or the floor, and at the same time a model evolves. It works like this: we are a team, and while one of us is putting the drawing down on paper the other is making the model. The model does not have a scale; like the drawing, it is intended to be a preliminary impression of the emergent building.

There are several reasons why we have evolved this design technique. One is certainly that we want to keep this design moment free of all material constraints, in order to arrive at a free ground-plan. The other reason is that we believe that architecture for our time must reflect the complexity and variety of modern society. We achieve this objective better with the method I have just described (which undoubtedly has more to do with art) than with the conventional one-dimensional design rules of today, which date from the nineteenth century. It seems important to us to replace this traditional way of thinking and seeing with a multilayered "logic" that allows us not only to understand complexity but also to invent it. We have described this process of design in a text written in 1989 and entitled "On the Razor's Edge":

When we speak of ships,
others think of shipwreckage.
We, however, think of wind-inflated
white sails.

When we speak of eagles,
the others think of a bird.
We, however, are talking about the
wing span.

When we speak of black panthers,
the others think of predatory animals.
We, however, think of the untamed
dangerousness of architecture.

When we speak of leaping whales,
others think of saurians.
We, however, think of 30 tons of
flying weight.
We won't find architecture in an
encyclopedia.
Our architecture can be found where
thoughts move faster than hands to
grasp it.

So the first drawing is immensely important for us, it is the first impression of a building.

*6. Heart Room
(Astroballoon),
1969*

In the last three to four years we have begun to shorten even further this very rapid design process, which can best be compared with coming close to the center of an explosion. We simply started to replace the spoken language, with which we were accustomed to communicate about the project, with the more rapid language of the body. That is, Helmut and I no longer talk; indications are enough, gestures. In 1987, when we won the competition for Melun Sénart, a satellite town for 240,000 inhabitants, body language was both the first drawing and the first model. So it was, too, in the project for the Ronacher Theater in Vienna, which I shall not discuss today.

At an early stage, in the late sixties, it was our concern to relate body and architecture. The Heart Room (fig. 6), for instance, which was designed and built in 1969 makes the heart-beat audible and visible. And in another project the sculpture translates the movements of the face, which are the natural façade of the emotions, into light and sound. In the Hard Space project of 1970 we triggered off explosions with our heart-beats.

Of course we did not invent this design technique from one day to the next, we practiced for a long time on installations, sculptures and objects. These installations are always an occasion for us to try things out, test new processes, or extend our plastic vocabulary. When we make such objects we never know what they can be used for. But it transpires that elements of these sculptures are later used as parts of our buildings.

The next project we called Architecture Is Now, because here for the first time the initial drawing became the object. The drawing, together with the model, was created on 5 March 1982. When we saw the finished model we were both horrified, and said, "It is so ugly that we just have to build it." We did build it, in a gallery in Stuttgart. The object consists of: a mobile part, which was made of steel and sheet metal; the walls were of concrete, cardboard and wood; and there was a bent rail arching over the entire project, breaking through the wall and ending in a wing.

In the project entitled The Skin of This City, which was built in Berlin in 1982, we were experimenting with urban sensuality. Hard and soft materials were stretched over spatial transversals. The Open House (fig. 7) was certainly a key project of this design method for us. For a long time we refused to design houses or apartments, simply because we did not want to determine the user's living-space. It was not until "open architecture" was "invented" that we were able to come closer to this theme.

We asked ourselves what a house might look like, but we never thought of rooms or details. We wanted to design the feeling, the feeling one would have when one entered the finished architecture. And our endless discussions were not aimed at determining the architectural ground-plan, they were intended to bring us closer to the psychological ground-plan. And suddenly the house was there; not as a building but

7. Open House, Malibu, California, 1983. Model

as a feeling. It was not the forms or the colors or the details that were important at that moment, but the feeling of the height, the feeling of the expansiveness, the curving out, even the view was there; one could feel it all. And in order not be distracted, not even by the act of drawing, the first drawing was made with our eyes closed. The fingers that touched the paper and the pencil were the seismograph of the feeling that this house would later radiate. At the same time the model was made; it was evolved step by step, and in the process it became evident that the seemingly arbitrary forms later certainly made sense. The tilted container, for instance, required a double-shell construction; on the one hand this is excellently suited to a passive energy concept, and on the other it permits us to move around the plumbing and wiring, wherever and whenever we want. For we were able to persuade the client to let us build only the shell for him; he was to live in that shell and find out where he wanted to sleep, where he wanted to read, where he wanted to sit, cook, and so on. For all this depends greatly on things one cannot necessarily see from the plans, the change of forms through light, for instance. So the client will move into the shell and not find any pre-determined rooms — only a single large space. He may subdivide it immediately, or he may never subdivide it. That is "open architecture."

In the initial stages structural planning is never an immediate priority, but it does become very important when the project is being realized, when the idea is being transposed into reality. Our statics expert, Oskar Gräf, always says that we build things that are a cross between a bridge and an aircraft. Actually, he is the Deconstructivist; he dissects the complicated and complex systems into separate parts in order to do the calculations.

The story of the Open House is actually a film story, and it needs a lecture to itself. At any rate the house is going to be built, in Malibu, California. You can see what it is like inside from the model. Whether we want to or not, we cannot get away from the California climate.

Now let me say something about what we understand by the "built drawing." It is easy to see that our drawings are not architectural draw-ings in the traditional sense, nor are they working drawings. They are the first capturing of the feeling on paper. The themes touched upon in the first drawing then become ever clearer and more visible as they are worked out.

The theme of the roof, for instance, had occupied us for a long time, and the commission to convert an attic into an attorney's office was therefore very welcome. The drawing opens up the theme: inside and outside, a contemporary corner solution, coming to terms with the context. The context is not defined here by proportion, material or color;

in this project the context is the relation between street and roof. Hence the inverted streak of lightning, which represents the line of energy that arches over the roof and tears it open (fig. 9).

Many people say that we are inordinately aggressive and that we destroy our architecture. This is an error, it is like confusing Deconstructivism and destruction. I believe it is wrong to speak of destruction. If we destroy something, like this old roof, for instance, it is only in order to create new spaces, spaces that are more differentiated and exciting than what was there before.

The task is easy to describe: 400 square meters of roof space were to be converted into an office, the main element being a central conference-room. One of our strategies was to plan and build the two side wings very economically, so as to direct all energy into the main part of the building. The two galleries — like balconies — one facing in, the other out, and separated by a glass wall and glass door — exemplify the concept of interplay between interior and exterior. A flight of stairs leads from the foyer up to the roof garden, which also gives access to the conference-room. However, the construction model shows that the translation of the spatial idea into architecture was not the simplest of tasks. When we showed the model in the Museum of Modern Art at the "Deconstructivist Architecture" exhibition in 1988, our American colleagues said, well, that's all very fine, but you won't want to build that. We had to laugh, for by then the building-work had already started.

It was important to us not just to roof over the central area with a simple glass cupola, we wanted to achieve a tense interplay between open and closed surfaces that would also serve to control light (fig. 8). We also considered very carefully what view we would facilitate and what view we would block. From the balcony that extends into the conference-room, for example, there is a view not only of the interior but also down into the street. Here one senses the backbone of the architecture, the flash of lightning that arches over the project.

One of the subsidiary supports breaks through the wall. This gave us the opportunity to design a light-slit through which, at certain times (if the sun is shining), an arrow of light will fall on the wall. In the evening the client can direct an artificial sun-arrow in the other direction.

In the side wings we made economical use of the existing construction to accommodate the whole project on a single level — no ramps, no stairs; the solution is reminiscent of Baron Münchhausen, who pulled himself out of the bog by his own hair.

I would like to give one last example of how we design details. The house administration wanted us to put windows in the prolongation of the staircase tower, but we thought the drawing with the windows was

too boring and so we simply crossed them out. Then we built the correction of the drawing.

We believe that one can never create a cleft between client and architect, for without the support of the client we could never have realized this project. However, I must admit that when we saw this building for the first time, a glittering diamond on the roof of the house, we were very proud just of ourselves.

To anticipate questions, we do not always make the first drawing for a project with our eyes closed, nor is this process always under pressure of time. In the Funder Works 3 project (1988/89) we tackled the theme very conceptually. We built the factory at the same time as the attic. The first approach was to let a factory do what it normally does, that is, produce. The shed was to be white and as free of detail as possible. The next step was to dissect out the parts that we saw as important and add to them, down to the condensed energy-center (fig. 10). The "dancing chimneys" in the center pose a "built question": Why do chimneys always have to stand straight? The production-shed, which is built very economically, is rendered plastic by additions or by leaving things out. We call one side of the neutral white shed the "100 km/h façade," because a freeway runs along it with cars traveling at such a speed. On the other side is a minor road, and here we have our "30 km/h façade" with the entrance; it is much more differentiated and broken up. And now the main entrance, easily recognized by its red color. There are many stories about this entrance (fig. 11). I will tell you one, to show you that we can keep our sense of humor even on large projects. During the building-work the problem of a fireproof wall arose here. We had no idea how to solve this until we discovered, on inspecting the building, that a complete stair-case had been wrongly installed. We had it ripped out, stood on its edge at the entrance and painted red, as a warning that architects' plans should be read more carefully.

An important principle for us is: "We believe nothing and no-one, because everyone is right, but nothing, really nothing, is right". But as we received the commission for this project on 24 December, we believe, or we are beginning to believe again, in Father Christmas.

Standing things on their edges and twisting them is actually a very simple principle of design, because it enables rigid functions to be broken up into spatially differentiated functions. We have also applied this principle in a project we are working on now. Again it is a factory, but not only a factory, it is a combination of a factory, an office and an apartment.

This tilting, twisting and turning that creates spaces one does not otherwise get is well illustrated in another project, a hundred-bed extension for the Hotel Altmannsdorf. The building, which otherwise would have run parallel to the street was twisted and turned to extend into the park. This twisting with concomitant supports enabled us to locate the hotel rooms at tree-top level. Of course we had another reason for doing

10. Funder-Werk 3, energy center with "dancing chimneys," St. Veit/Glan, Austria, 1988—89

*11. Funder-Werk 3,
glass corner with
entrance on the
right, 1988 – 89*

this — we could not build at ground level because the building floats above a lake. By tilting one story of what is basically a three-story slab we acquired a fourth floor, which we were able to use as a leisure area. The whole is 60 meters long and it juts out 30 meters.

With the project for an office building in Lower Austria, one can see very clearly that tilting and twisting gives us spaces that may be not only more differentiated, but also more interesting than if one thought in terms of one box within another. (By the way, it is very amusing when Rem Koolhaas says: "You people at Himmelblau are too sculptural for my taste, I am pragmatic, I only build cubes, for that is abstract and logical." We hope he has fun!) This tilting creates spaces beneath the buildings that can be opened up to the sourrounding area. Similarly, the two office sections are pushed apart in order to integrate exterior space. One can walk through the buildings from the cellar to the roof. A ramp-like access permits people to move from the entrance across the roofs into the presentation and training room. One ramp, like that in the attic I mentioned before, projects into the room. The theme of the cut-out form, the cross or "x" I could almost say, has been occupying us more and more recently.

As you know, architecture needs at least three supports in order to stand firm. We noticed that in the last few projects we had started questioning that third support. What we were interested in was movement. We designed a mobile kitchen, for example, with adjustable tables and swinging or pull-out parts (fig. 12).

Mobility continues to play a large role in our projects as can be seen in Walden, designed in 1968, and in the competition project for the

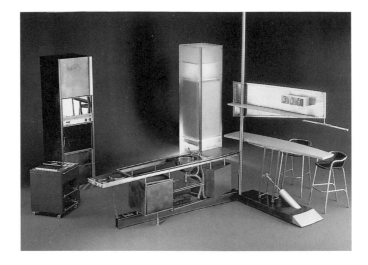

12. Mal-Zeit kitchen, 1990. Prototype for EWE

media museum in Karlsruhe, where red parts indicate mobility. The logical consequence is that whole spaces move, as in the project for Japan, the Jasmac Bar Building for Fukuoka (1989; fig. 1). It is perhaps worth mentioning how we got this job. Some guy phoned from Tokyo and asked, "Do you want to build a restaurant?" I thought, another restaurant, oh God, well, why not? We met in Tokyo, the client sat opposite us with a pile of Coop Himmelblau publications and said, well, the restaurant should look like this, and so on, it should have interpenetrations and wings. This is the building it is to be located in. I saw a Postmodern project and said, no, impossible. I started to talk, I talked and talked and talked, and he said, alright, what do you want to build? And I said, we want houses with flying roofs, frozen stairs, burning walls. He looked at me and said, let's do it. And I thought, that's what you say, we've heard that a thousand times before. No, he said, just a moment, and pulled a Filofax out of his pocket. You know what a Filofax is, a megadiary for managers. This one was like a bound book, very thick, but here was no diary inside, there were hundreds of city plans, from Sydney to Toronto, and on all of them there were areas marked in red. He leafed through them and said, the red areas all belong to me. You should build it here — would you like to? We said yes, of course. The man snapped his fingers, a photographer appeared, we both smiled and were photographed. And that was the contract.

We designed the model for Fukuoka, but we were not able to go to Tokyo and present it. So we made a Video in Los Angeles, and our Japanese project architect explained it all in Japanese. Then we got a letter back saying the project was so fantastic that Fukuoka was too small, it would have to be in Sapporo. So there it is in Sapporo, a bar and restaurant building. It has seven bars, and the mobile part is the glass cube that can be hired for private functions. It moves through the roof, and gives a view over the whole city. Each of these bars was to be different, and so we covered the floors with a sheet of glass, because we imagine they will be developed as sculpture to emphasize the character of each bar. There is also a special space that goes right through the whole building and breaks through the roof. The client was very skeptical when he saw our attic conversion in Vienna. The Japanese always want bar and restaurant buildings without windows, that is, with solid walls. Our response took the form of two façades. The front façade is of aluminum and is completely closed. The elements that pierce it like arrows are the signs for this bar building. Inside they form the constructive elements, which support the entire body of the bar and the fittings. On the left the fire-escape moves diagonally upwards. And for the right lateral façade we have proposed a huge drawing. But as this is a work of art we have to protect the picture with a skin of structural glazing.

The project for a mixed-use building in Los Angeles (Melrose; fig. 13) also has mobile parts. It is a combination of restaurant, bars, bookshop and boutiques. A glass tower stands on the corner site. It has not static platforms, but bars instead, which move continuously. This mobile architecture is in stark contrast to the architecture of Los Angeles, where basically only boxes are built. This is understandable, because the economic pressure is very great. Admittedly, once they have been built, the boxes only stand for about five years. We are trying to find an answer

13. Melrose I, bar and office buildings, Los Angeles, 1990

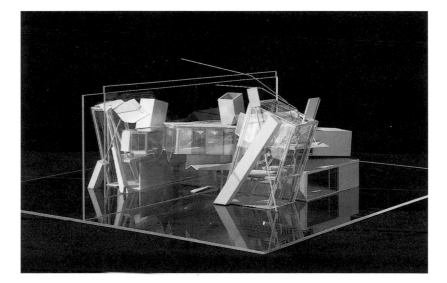

to how one can fragment these crates with our method of twisted sections so as to achieve the image that is essential for success in this city.

We also built a pavilion, now called "Folly," for Groningen, a city in Holland which runs a show of video-clips in the autumn. Many of our friends were also invited to build pavilions. We were able to choose the video program, and we chose Rock 'n 'Roll and Sex. That's why the auditorium opens and closes; it closes when Rock 'n 'Roll is being shown.

It is very easy to explain Deconstructivism: architecture must blaze. It is an explanation for Deconstructivism, which should not be confused with destruction. Flame stands not only for burning, flame is for us the paradigm of open architecture.

It all started in 1968. That was when architecture exploded. In the mid-seventies, with the advent of Postmodernism, our projects became ever more angry and cynical. While others, around 1978, were drawing houses with columns and attic stories and tympana, we were inventing houses to be built of raw concrete, pierced by an arrow at the end of which a flame-wing ignites.

In 1980 we drew with a lighter. And at the end of 1980 things really started to burn. We organized the action "Flame-Wing" (fig. 14) in Graz. The flame-wing is 15 meters high and weighs five tons. It is installed in the courtyard of the Technical University.

ARCHITECTURE MUST BLAZE (1980)

*You can judge just how bad
the 70's were when you look
at its super tense architecture.*

*Opinion polls and a com-
placent democracy live behind
Biedermeier-facades.*

*But we don't want to build
Biedermeier. Not now and at
no other time.
We are tired of seeing Palladio
and other historical masks.
Because we don't want
architecture to exclude everything that is disquieting.*

*We want architecture to have
more. Architecture that bleeds,
that exhausts, that whirls and
even breaks. Architecture that
lights up, that stings, that rips,
and under stress tears.
Architecture should be cavern-
ous, firey, smooth, hard,
angular, brutal, round, delicate,
colorful, obscene, voluptuous,
dreamy, alluring, repelling, wet,
dry and throbbing. Alive or
dead. Cold — then cold as a block of ice.
Hot — then hot as a blazing wing.
Architecture must blaze.*

Peter Eisenman

STRONG FORM, WEAK FORM

Architecture has traditionally been a strong form discipline. This is usually taken to mean that there is a one-to-one correlation between meaning and function, meaning and structure, meaning and form. As a strong form discipline, architecture is also a very problematic discipline, because it has a weak condition of sign: in other words, it does not have a system of explicit signs. It is difficult to express happiness, sadness, goodness, badness — any emotional or philosophic concept. What language can deal with, architecture cannot. Language is also a strong form system. There is a very direct correlation between the word "wolf" and a person named Wolf. But we realize in language that "wolf" means not only that person, but many other people and many other nuances in language other than an animal. For example, it is a person who chases women. They sometimes meet and overlap, these "wolfs." Language also has a symbolic connotation, where there is not a one-to-one correspondence between word and sign. Literature and poetry try to make opaque the transparent relationship between sign and signified. On the other hand, in journalism, when we read the newspaper we read for clarity. It is edited for clarity, for a strong relationship between sign and signified.

When we read literature, like Shakespeare, we are not reading for clarity but rather for the possible opacity in the language. Because when we read Shakespeare, we already know the story, we know the history of Henry V, we know the history of Romeo and Juliet, we have read the story in some other form before. So we are not reading to understand. Language has a very clear way of representing opacity, in literature and in poetry. But in architecture, sign and signified have always been together; function, symbolism, aesthetic form have always been merged, not separated, whereas in traditional views of language they have been separated.

In traditional structuralist thought the signified and the signifier are seen as separate entities. Poststructuralism says, however, that these two

1. *Wexner Center, Center for the Visual Arts, Ohio State University, Columbus, 1982 – 89*

have always been together. Now this is just like the situation in architecture, because in architecture they have always been together. Thus in architecture, in order to find a transparency in this given opacity, in order to have a possibility for a multiplicity of meanings, one has to pull the sign and signifier apart. One has to pull apart the one-to-one relationship between structure, form, meaning, content, symbolism, etc., so that it is possible to make many meanings. This pulling apart is what I call a displacement. Vienna is the city where displacement and ideas of displacement obviously were born through Sigmund Freud; so the concept of displacement is not a new one.

The question is, why do we want to displace architecture today? Why is it necessary to separate function and structure from symbolism, meaning, and form? Because in the past architecture always symbolized reality. In other words, while language was one kind of reality, poetry another, music another, architecture was perhaps the ultimate condition of reality, because it dealt with physical facts, with bricks and mortar, house and home. It was physical place, the fundamental condition of reality.

The cosmology that we exist in has changed. In the fourteenth century there was a change from a theocentric cosmology to an anthropocentric one. It changed in the nineteenth century from an anthropocentric one to a technocentric one, to a mechanical view of the world — that is, a scientific, mathematical, rational view of the world. This lasted through the Second World War. After the Second World War the cosmology again changed: the mechanistic, technocentric world became an informational world, one ordered by electronics; it is now a world of media.

Let me give you a few examples of this changed view of reality. In the televising of sports there is something which is called "instant replay." This means that a good play is played over again, a goal is shown in four different ways. My children grew up as "instant replay junkies." Because of this they have lost the faculty of watching a real game. As a matter of fact, they are more interested in the commercials (and in a mediated world, maybe the commercials are better). Thus reality changed, reality became the instant replay and the commercials. The eating habits of my children also changed. They would say we need to eat at McDonald's, then they would change to Wendy's. Basically, they were eating commercials. In other words, it did not matter whether the meat was good or bad, they were not eating the meat, actually, but the commercials. When there is no instant replay at the game, they do not know how to watch that reality.

But this has been corrected now in the United States. First they had huge television screens in the stadium, on which you could watch instant replay. And then they realized there was something better than instant replay — you could actually have a big television screen, but huge, like the size of this wall here, and you could actually watch the game on television at the game, complete with instant replay. And, in fact, I went to a game, a baseball game, in Chicago last week with my girlfriend and she said, "Peter, now tell me the truth, what are you going to do, watch the game or the television?" And it's really interesting, I thought I would watch the game — and we had very good seats, we were close to the baseball players, etc. — but I realized after a while, my eyes aren't so good, it was much better to watch on the television, right? And now they even have the commercials. So that people are getting up at the game, when the game is on, and coming back in between to watch the commercials. It's a fantastic thing that's happened. People now come with binoculars to watch like this — but they're watching the television.

You wonder what's reality. You go to a race-track and there is a big screen with what is called simulcast. Simulcast means you can watch a horserace from anywhere in the country when you are not watching the horserace where you are. The problem is that the giant screen covers up the far straight. So that when you are watching a real horserace and you are standing down by the track, the horses run by, they go around the second turn, down the backstretch, and they disappear behind the TV screen. They immediately appear on TV as soon as they disappear and you are left wondering what is going on back there. Something is on TV, and then they are coming out again around the third turn. And you wonder whether they have gone down into a chute and others have come out. Or have they substituted other horses? Anything could have happened. The television could have been prerecorded to look like the race. Who knows?

Speaking of reality, I went to a Monday night football game which was on national television. It happened to be also at the time of the last game of our baseball World Series. So everybody in the audience had a portable TV, right? Or things with ears. And it was like a bunch of Martians sitting there. And they were listening to something else. And the players were sort of poised, ready to play. When someone hit a home run in the other stadium, and a huge instantaneous roar went up in the crowd, a roar like what happens when a play begins. And one of the teams jumped offside, and they threw the flag and said penalty, when nothing had happened, because something happened in a stadium fifty miles away. So you begin to realize that the media invade our world in a very interesting way.

Let's talk about food. McDonald's. McDonald's is omnipresent. You now have McDonald's in — I don't know about Vienna yet — but you have McDonald's in Italy, etc., and everybody wants to eat at McDonald's. Now, I would call fast food strong food. That is, it reduces the possibility of cuisine to something very simple — and direct. So most people, all they know how to do now is eat hamburgers, french fries, etc. So McDonald's have gotten very clever. They've added to fast food, they've now begun to homogenize tacos, Chinese food, pasta. You can go and have all kinds of things now, but all reduced to a very simple formula.

What this has done is brought about what is called, I suppose here as well, *nouvelle cuisine, nuova cucina* in Italian. And what *nuova cucina* is, is a reaction to fast food, in other words, to strong food. *Nuova cucina* is: you don't know what you're eating any more. You go in a very fancy restaurant in Milan and you say you want *prosciutto melone*. And they look at you kind of ... you know. Now, *prosciutto melone* used to be a very sophisticated thing to eat in a restaurant. And they say, you know, you want *prosciutto melone*, you go to McDonald's. So I said, O.K., what about a little *pasta alla carbonara*? You know, I was thinking, maybe speak a little Italian, I thought this was really very exotic pasta. And they said, "We don't have that any more." No more *pasta alla carbonara*? They said, "Well, look at the menu." And I used to be able to speak a little Italian, I mean more or less, but you don't know what these things are. You look at these things, and I would ask my friends who are Italians, "What is this kind of pasta?" "I don't know what it is." And the things come out and you don't know if you're eating pasta or fish or brains or whatever. It's all sort of mixed together, in a very strange way. This is what I call weak food, because you don't know what you're eating any more. And this is what everybody wants. They want something, they don't know what.

My son is a disc-jockey in very exotic nightclubs in New York City: Mars, Morrisey, etc. And what he does is he scratches records. What is scratching? To take the structures of rock or pop music, and take their strong forms away — that is, the rhythm, the harmonics, the melody, the narrative sound — and produce in essence weak music. In other words, something with no bass, no melody, no harmony.

And hundreds of people move to this music which he creates. It is of a particular moment in time. It has lost its condition of narrative time, which is something repeatable or static in time. It is now no longer repeatable. It is now about music as performance, as event. And what we realize is that the time of narrative, that is, moving from here to there as a rational discourse, in music, in the latest music that people are listening to, has been replaced by another structure.

This guy, my son, has a collection of records, each week he's got to buy a hundred new records, because the people don't want to hear the same scratched stuff the next week. So he has to "remix" every week, because they do not tape it and save it. It is all prima. That is the essence of going to a discotheque to have something of the original. But this is a different kind of original from what Walter Benjamin meant when he spoke of "the aura of the original of the work of art," it's now the original of mechanical reproduction, it is the original of media. It is mediated originality without. And no longer is the time of reality the time of stasis, the time of history, the time of this room. It is a different kind of time, the time of the event.

For example, in the past a news conference was something where somebody was to say something important. And people came to hear something that was real. Now a news conference is set up for the ten o'clock news. The ten o'clock news has got certain time-slots called "sound bites" — fifteen seconds, twenty seconds, thirty seconds. So the President, before he speaks, is mediated by his consultants to say something in a certain fifteen-second period that the television people will put on the nightly news. The rest does not matter. Because all people hear is what is on TV. They do not read any more. In fact now we have newspapers that are formated like television.

All of this makes one understand that reality has become mediated. Now people can no longer even watch minute-long commercials. Now they are fifteen seconds. Now in one minute you are getting four different commercials. The condensation, another Freudian term, is so strong that it only takes fifteen seconds to deploy it. And when one is hit with information at fifteen-second intervals, that is real condensation.

Now the ad industry has decided that in order to get people, they have got to go to weak form. My friend, who is a commercial photographer, used to do Coca-Cola, Seagram, etc. and of course the central thing in the photograph was the Coca-Cola bottle or the Seagram bottle or whatever bottle. Now they blur the Coca-Cola bottle. Everything else is beautifully in focus and the Coca-Cola bottle is out of focus. It is blurred. It's a commercial for Energizer batteries. It's a pink rabbit that comes out banging a drum. But it comes out during somebody else's commercial. You're sitting and you're watching for almost a minute something for sneakers, Adidas, or something like this.

Architecture's reality needs to be reconsidered to stand in a mediated world. To do that means to displace the conditions of architecture as they used to be. In other words, the condition that saw architecture as reasonable, as understandable, as clearly functioning. Now this displacement does not mean that architecture should not function. Rather, the displacement concerns the conditions of architecture as defined by Vitruvius.

Vitruvius said that a building had to have *Utilitas, firmitas, venustas.* Which literally means utility, firmness, pleasingness. But he did not mean it should function well, because all buildings function well, or that it should be structured well, or that it should contain well, or that it should be aesthetically well. What he meant was, it should "look like" it functions well; it should look like it is built well, etc. Thus, he permanently elided actual function and symbolic function in what I call a "strong form" relationship. When Le Corbusier said, "A house is a machine to live in," he did not mean it should really be a machine, because basically he was building bourgeois houses with nineteenth-century functions. He meant that the house should look like a machine. And so they built an ordinary house with all the ordinary functions and made it look like a machine.

2. Wexner Center, Center for the Visual Arts, Ohio State University, Columbus, 1982–89

What I am suggesting is that, yes, a building has to function, but it does not have to look like it functions. Yes, a building has to stand up, but it does not have to look like it stands up. And when it does not look like it stands up, or it does not look like it functions, then it functions

3. Wexner Center, Center for the Visual Arts, Ohio State University, Columbus, 1982 – 89

and stands differently. Now when I did a museum for the Wexner Center in Columbus, Ohio, I said, "We have to exhibit art, but do we have to exhibit art the way art has been traditionally exhibited, that is, against a neutral background? Because," I said, "You know, art has always been critical of life, that is what gave art its potency, its poetry. And architecture should serve art, in other words, be a background for art? Absolutely not," I said, "Architecture should challenge art and this notion that it should be a background."

And the proof of this, for me, is that in Cincinnati, where I am doing what I think is an important building, they just had a recent show of Robert Mapplethorpe's photographs, and they are about to lock up the director. They are having a trial, a pornography trial in Cincinnati, trying to prove, which they will prove, that the director is a pornographer. I have been desperately wishing someone would put me on trial as a pornographer, me the architect, right? And maybe try and put me into jail. Because no one cares. Because we accommodate, we allow, we never critique society, or art, or life; we accommodate life, we accommodate art, we roll over. You have never heard of one architect being threatened because his or her work was politically active, that is, it threatened anybody. Most people do not care. Yet poets get locked up, artists get locked up. You know, William Butler Yeats brought about the Irish Rebellion. Corbu? They did not care. They used him. He even went and begged Mussolini to give him work. He would have begged anybody so as to build.

What I am saying is that we need to displace this concept of architecture as a service, as an accommodating profession, as one that people

inhabit. Just the notion of inhabit means "to grow used to". And the habitual is what people want from an architect. In other words, architecture is O.K. as long as it indulges the habits of people. But once you question the habit, that is, the way museum curators show works, the way art critics write about works in a museum, you upset the balance, you cause a stir. The art critics hate my Wexner Center building. The curators hate it. Why? Because it provokes them to have to think again about the relationship between painting and the space of painting. Because they cannot hang easel-paintings on the walls of my building. And yet, what is interesting is that artists are talking about recontextualizing art.

If you remember, Michelangelo's work was in a context, it was not to be put in a museum. They did not scrape Michelangelo, Giulio Romano, the Carraccis off the walls and hang them in museums, they painted in situ. Art was in situ. Artists are now saying they want art to be in situ. That is, they want to take painting off the easel and sculpture off the pedestal and make it site-specific. Except when it comes to galleries and museums. Then the most radical artist wants architecture to roll over and be a pedestal and an easel. And architects are all too willing to provide pedestals and easels for artists. We need to rethink this idea of architecture.

Now, what to do about it? In school — let me tell you how corrupt the relationship between student and teacher is: basically it is "don't bother me if I don't bother you." The teacher comes in, and the first day

5. Cincinnati University, new design and extension, Cincinnati, Ohio, 1988. Model

of the design studio says, "We are going to design a library." And not one student says, "Why? Why a library? Why not a school, or a jail, or a zoo?" There's no questioning. Maybe a smattering of grumbling. They are not going to be library specialists. Students never ask why they study structures, by the way, or why they study mechanical engineering in an architectural curriculum.

I have never designed a structure — I do not need to know anything about it. I failed structures, as you probably could tell from my buildings, but it does not matter, because I am not allowed to design a structure in the United States or I would be sued, right? I have to hire a structural engineer, a mechanical engineer. So why waste time? Better to study Latin, you know? Leon Krier would have been a much better architect if he'd studied Latin instead of . . . .

So then the teacher says, "We are going to do research. Go and research libraries." As if you needed to research libraries to do a library. But it has been decided that the history of libraries influences what we should do today. In other words, that the way to learn about libraries is to research not just the architecture of libraries, but how books are made, how they are checked out, how they are processed, stored, etc. Who needs to know these things? There are consultants to tell you about all that. I do not know how a library works. If I were going to do a library I would go hire somebody who knew what libraries were about — as I did when we did the convention center. Who knows what happens in a convention center? We did one just now, and a convention center consultant told me this is what it had to be. I said, "Gee, that doesn't influence the architecture at all, really. I can do whatever I want." And they said, "Sure, go ahead." And I did.

So basically, the study of program is useless. In any case, let us assume now that the student brings the project in, and the teacher first of all says, "Why did you do this?" And the student will start to answer why he or she did this, "Well, because I needed to have a clear entry. I needed to have a clear circulation system. I needed to show what the building symbolically meant in the street. I needed to respond, I needed to respond, I needed to respond." Right? And if the student gets all of the responses right, that is, clear and reasonable, the teacher will say, "That's good." Even though it may be horrible-looking. As long as all the answers are "motherhood" answers, it is O.K. *You* try as a student to answer a teacher when he says, "Why did you do that?" with, "I don't know." Or, "It doesn't matter why I did it." Or, "What does it mean?" "I have no idea. You make it up." These kinds of responses would mean expulsion from any school, anywhere.

Architecture has a serious problem. Advances in science have always been made because someone did not believe what the teacher was telling them. They did not believe, in fact, in the principle of the non-loss of materiality, they did not believe in the notion of narrative time. They did not believe in the philosophical terms of teleology or ontology, or even typology. The only way to advance in a discipline is to displace knowledge. And the only discourses that remain healthy are those that are displacing discourses. The ones that cling to their theory and their tradition and their rationality, die. Now architecture may already be dead. I do not know. I do not think anybody cares. As long as people make money in building what sells, they will be published anyway, because public relations people will make sure they get published, because journalists have to have something to write about. Media in the end is debilitating. Because what we all want, media, is the killer of creativity in any time.

Because these guys need to be mediated so much — because the press keeps saying, "We want something new, do you have anything new for us?" And they keep getting more work only to stay — to stay real. Because they assume that "the image" in the media is their reality. And if they lose that, it is like losing their shadow. They are so desperate, we are so desperate, that we cannot work any more. Society often has no satisfaction from the actual product of our labor, people are only interested in the mediated result.

Weak form derives from several ideas: that there is no single truth; that there is no decidability (things have to be undecidable, arbitrary);

that things are no longer essential (there is no essence to architecture, there is no essence to anything); that it is all in the excess. If you look at David Lynch it is about excess. If you look at anything in contemporary discourse, it is about the condition of excess, that is, nothing relying on essence. Weak form is arbitrary, undecidable, excessive, and has no ontology or teleology of value; that is, no strong relationship to narrative space or time.

7. *Carnegie Mellon University,
Research Center, Pittsburgh,
Pennsylvania, 1988. Model*

6. *Casa Guardiola, detached family house,
Puerto de Santa Maria, Cadiz,
Spain, 1987. Model*
8. *Pittsburgh Technology Center, 1988. Model*

9. Hotel
En Banyoles,
Hotel Design
Competition,
Gerona, Spain,
1988. View of
north side

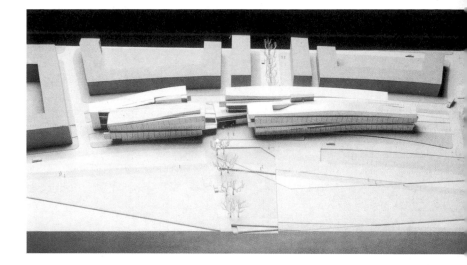

10. Hotel
En Banyoles,
Hotel Design
Competition,
Gerona, Spain,
1988. Model

11. Koizumi Sangyo Building, office building,
Tokyo, Japan, 1988. Model

12. Columbus Convention Center,
Columbus, Ohio, 1988. Model

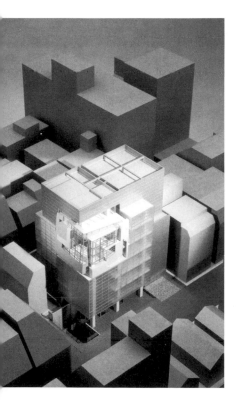

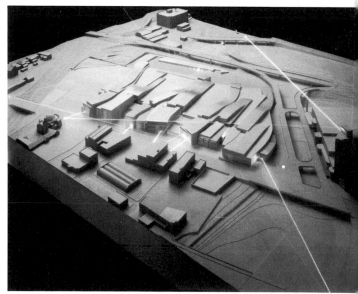

Zaha Hadid

RECENT WORK

When I won the Hong Kong Peak competition in 1983 a lot of people thought I had just emerged from the Iraqi desert, but I had in fact been living in London for some time, working and teaching at the Architectural Association. I feel that the work I did before the Peak was really very critical and essential to the build-up of that project. The controversy surrounding a show hosted at the Museum of Modern Art in New York two years ago also contributed to this impression. The controversy arose due to the curiosity of the public and the fact that the host of the show was Philip Johnson. There was a very strenuous connection between the notion of Constructivism and Deconstruction as a philosophical issue.

During my fourth year as a student at the AA, I began to look at Suprematism and the idea that it had never been tested in architecture before but was known only as a movement in painting and sculpture. Through a project given to us by my tutors Elia Zenghelis and Rem Koolhaas, we began a route of investigations which led to the work we are doing now.

This is not a royal 'we'. I used this 'we' in Germany and they thought I was a princess — I am not a princess at all; we are a group of people in London and it is the work of ex-students who are now collaborators of mine. It's not just me sitting in a cell producing this work.

The project they gave us was the Malevich Tektonik. The idea was that this form — if given a dimension, scale, context, and location and then incorporated into a program — could become an architecture. The early studies of the Malevich tektonik were superimposed on a London bridge and articulated horizontally through a series of floor-like plates. Thus began the understanding of the whole notion of Suprematism and how it was to be integrated into architecture, how its degree of dynamic could be interpreted in architecture, how the plan could be developed in a new way. The whole notion of fragmentation implied that the rules given to architects and architectural students were no longer valid.

---

1. Kurfürstendamm, Berlin, 1987.
Office building, view of fire wall

Obviously one would question the value of rediscovering Suprematism in the mid seventies. We felt at the time that although it was very important to be able to invent new programs and to rewrite the program for architecture, and although the spirit of the early twentieth century was that of optimism, we were confronted, in the seventies, with this notion that there was no progress in architecture and that we could only go forward by looking to the past. We felt that we had to examine this culture of twentieth-century Modernism very carefully — for example, by looking at the very early projects done by Leonidov.

The Russian Revolution brought a new way of life that demanded a new program, a new work ethos, unusual leisure facilities and a collision of all these things in a modern urban context. Take Leonidov's Ministry of Heavy Industry on Red Square, where despite the historical significance of the place, a modern solution was thinkable. This idea of juxtaposition of the new and the old became very interesting to us. One could almost see it as a kind of contextual architecture but it had to do with a superimposition of the new on the old so that both could co-exist.

Another example is the RCA Building in Rockefeller Center, New York — one of the most intense urban developments. One thing that I always liked about this building was its name — the RCA — and its lettering which went very well with the architecture. Now it's been sold to the Japanese and it's called the GE Building. To my disappointment there are now GEs plastered all over it.

The idea common to both the Russians and the Americans was a new synthetic condition in urbanism. The Radio City Music Hall was supposed to simulate sunrise and sunset and feelings of spring, summer, fall, or winter by using different aromas. So it was the making of a new living condition in an enclosed environment. In New York this idea developed into very elaborate lobbies, which became an extension of the civic section of the city. These are not private spaces — you can walk through the city from one lobby to the next.

These are issues that confronted us when we did the Hong Kong Peak. The Peak is a pivot in my career, a very important project for me. It has to do with the notion of layering and geological discovery in terms of program — a layering of one's previous education and all the intentions one had.

Hong Kong is a very interesting condition. It's set off the shore from the mainland, Kowloon. The first layer is synthetic land, the second layer on a hill is much more congested and the Peak itself is the highest point of the mountain. I had been to Hong Kong a year before. I felt from the beginning that any intervention upon this condition could not be vertical, but had to be horizontal. It also had to have a degree of sharp-

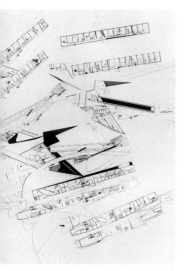

2. *Hong Kong Peak, 1982. Ground plan*

3. *Hong Kong Peak, 1982 – 83. Overall isometric*

ness — like a blade cutting through the mountain. When you ascend the mountain away from the city the congestion lessens and the towers of the city begin to fragment across what is called the Mid-levels. The top is almost isolated — that is where the project slides in. As the object is placed on Hong Kong it begins to violate and change the city.

We decided to re-write the brief of the competition. In a sense we broke the rules but actually we just twisted them. This gave us the possibility of doing the whole project on one piece of land. We let the beams journey, flying across the mountains. As they crossed them, they began to interfere with the rock and land. At the point of interference what is removed as rock from the mountain is replaced by a new architecture (figs. 2, 3), so that the project is very geological in a way.

Each of the four beams has a very specific program. We felt that the club facility in the centre cannot become a private condition but a civic space which is part of the city of Hong Kong. The core is thus a kind of void, suspended between the top two beams and lower two beams; we see it as a metropolitan resort, directly related to the crowded and congested city but at the same time removed from its context.

The lower beams which are inserted into the rock contain studios and a hotel on two floors, the top two beams private apartments; it gets more and more private as you move up. A raised deck incorporates the swimming pool and sports facilities of the club. A ramp connects the Peak to the existing roadway, because all the rock has been taken away and replaced by a third beam with patio houses.

These colliding beams approximate living conditions in a city. All the programs are very close to each other, and there is no segregation between the elements.

The idea is that you do not fortify the site and in that sense there is no privacy within the central zone of the Peak.

The Peak is predominantly shrouded in mist, so you often cannot see anything outside the site. Thus, the site elements are in effect landscape. As you enter you see how the land has been carved out — seven meters of rock have been taken away. The point of arrival, which also has the secondary supports, is a pivot: you can take the ramp up to the library or you can go inside the club. In the library you can see the polished surfaces of the floor against the ruggedness of the landscape, and the movement of the cars against the movement of the swimmers in the pool. On the terrace you see the earth cascading towards the polished surfaces; the swimming-pool and the paraboloids — the only things which have a certain fluidity within the project — are set in motion as a result.

In 1988 we were asked to do a project for "Berlin 2,000." Everybody was doing projects going over the Wall and under the Wall, but I started from the premise that by the year 2,000 the Wall would have disappeared, and we would have to find something appropriate for a reunited city.

In 1986 I was asked to do two projects at almost the same time. One was for IBA housing and the other a competition. The site where all the IBA housing projects were to be inserted was very near the Wall. I had gone to Berlin with this incredible enthusiasm, thinking this is the city of Mies van der Rohe and Ludwig Hilberseimer, but instead I was confronted by an intense degree of cuteness and was reminded constantly

4. Internationale Bauausstellung Berlin, 1986 – 87. House, perspective view

5. Internationale Bauausstellung Berlin, 1986 – 87 House

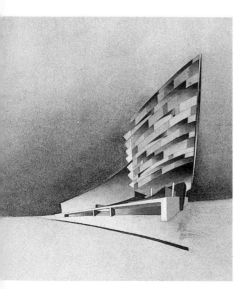
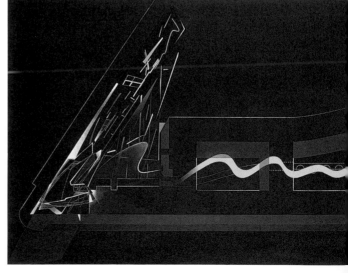

that this was what the people wanted. So I had a big dilemma as to how to deal with the situation.

After many, many meetings they told us which site we had. They were very kind to me; they gave me a triangular site because they thought I liked triangles. They told us this was a very homogeneous condition and therefore it had to be only three stories high. When I looked at the site there was nothing homogeneous about it; they told us we should not look at the hotel, just pretend it was not there, because it was ugly. So the guiding force for the height of the site was the church. I always made faces and frowned, so they said mine could be five stories. So I asked was that an average? I spoke no German, which is a good thing sometimes. I don't speak Japanese or German, so I can always pretend that I don't understand what they are saying. They always say we didn't understand what you asked us so the contract is wrong, and so on. So I played the same game. I asked was it an average of five stories? And they said yes. After many trials and errors we had two buildings. One is a corner-building — because a tower is bad news — and the other is a long building (figs. 4, 5). One is eight stories high and one is three, averaging at five and a half. So I had half a story to bargain for. Again that was crazy, but I said you did tell me in writing it was an average of five and that was that, as far as I was concerned. The corner-building is still moving; they expect a high migration of East Berliners to the western part so they now want to make the "tower" much taller.

The site was initially intended for women architects. I thought this was like a leper colony and that it was ridiculous. So they said okay, we'll invite some Russian architects. The Russians at that time never responded and so it was just me and two other women, one Israeli and one Berliner, and three Polish architects. It was a very happy marriage between the Poles and the women.

All the projects have a perimeter block that's three stories high. Ours has this thing on the corner, which is supposed to imply a new kind of apartment for younger people; they are like lofts, with few divisions.

From there we moved on to a much less clinical condition — that of Kurfürstendamm (figs. 1, 6). It's an office building. It must be the smallest office building — two point seven meters wide by fifteen meters long. We cantilevered over the road so that the project would be slightly less cramped. It was interesting to see how we could deal with a condition where the site was so confined and where all the services had to be accommodated within the site — the staircases and the elevators as well as the mechanical, engineering and structural systems. We felt that the only way to deal with this situation and the site was to not occupy the ground by a corridor; the ground floor had a different quality and led more to the street.

The building needed a degree of lightness and therefore the landing was very critical. It also had to become an extension of the street and the corner.

We had to do one tricky thing — move the stairs from the ground floor to the first floor so that the staircases never coincided. By just shifting the walls we were left with extra space, despite the smallness of the site. The site was taken away from a long corridor condition and released back into the city. This project was in a way very intriguing because it required intense precision, and also implied that you could still release space and make something interesting despite the tightness.

It has two sequences — one horizontal and one vertical. The horizontal one is the build-up of the structural walls, which starts from a new firewall and is squished or sandwiched behind a glass curtain wall. The vertical sequence shows how the build-up of the vertical elements occurs — fundamentally the three structural walls because of the shift in the condition of the plan, which then cantilevers or suspends as a box the offices. So the offices have no division — they have a linear quality and are much more fluid.

This project caused a lot of controversy. We won it in 1987 but the client wanted Helmut Jahn. Because they gave us planning permission, so the story goes, Helmut Jahn had to abide by our profile. Fundamentally he just copied the building and put it there.

When you see the building from the front (fig. 5) it's behind the glass curtain wall and from the back there is a slit between the new firewall and the second structural wall. Through that gap is suspended this new room at the top which hangs over you as you enter the site. The gap is in effect the entrance.

The curtain wall peels away from the façade, so there is a constant gap between the glass wall and the floors. This gap became a glass floor.

The front is very transparent and the back is very solid. The structural tie is the staircase, which in a way ties the two walls together: the central shaft is all staircase. The staircase shaft also shifts, so the staircase never lands, it transfers on the first floor.

About six months after we did this, we were visited by a group of Japanese developers. There were fifteen of them, and they asked me whether I wanted to build something in Japan. I said yes, not taking it terribly seriously. They asked, did I mind doing something small, and I said it couldn't be smaller than the Ku'damm building. So I showed them the model we had — they said nothing — I gave them posters of the Ku'damm project as a present, and they went away. Three months

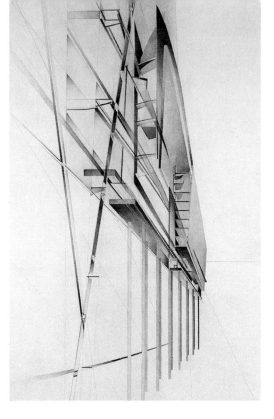

*6. Kurfürsten-
damm, Berlin,
1987. Office
building, exploded
perspective*

later they came back to us and said yes, we would like you to do something in Japan, and to my total shock the site was smaller. Since then I've been inundated with very small sites; there is in fact one that starts from zero.

Berlin was interesting because the leftover sites were a result of WW2 bombs; the new streets were laid out arbitrarily, so one was left with very peculiar sites. Tokyo has peculiar sites because of the incredible congestion and the lack of land. Now they have the engineering and the science to build thirty stories below ground as well as a thousand meters above ground.

One site is four meters wide and fifteen meters long and the other is more generous — it is eight meters wide at the top after cantilevering. It's supposed to slide into a canyon of buildings. From the beginning it had to have two kinds of divisions; it had to have a wall that allowed one area for free circulation and the other for retail use. The number of stories in relation to the number of square meters and total height never correlate.

The space that was left after putting in all the walls and the structure for earthquakes was two meters in total. It meant just a staircase and a lift. What then became more and more prominent was this dividing wall between the area for free movement and the usable area. It became what we called the metal wall, which is a blade that slices the site almost in half. It was increasingly clear that the site was becoming a giant solid wall, as it was made up of so many walls (figs. 7, 8). We felt that the congestion of Tokyo required an area to be released back to the city — so we had to carve away a lump out of these walls and make it into a space.

The building is carved out of the ground; you go over a glass bridge to get to it. There is a pit; you enter under a canopy and you can go up or down to the various floors. The first wall is made of concrete, the second of metal, and the last of glass. Because the height restrictions are not consistent we were able to have four normal floors (the maximum number of floors being five) and one story ten meters tall. So in the centre of the space is a room two meters wide, fifteen meters long, and ten meters tall. We felt that the target of the project was to create a space in Tokyo where you could really breathe. The idea was that the site exaggerates the congestion of the city, so that when you are released into this room you gasp in relief.

On one side of the site is a blue curtain wall which suspends over you as you enter the building. As it moves towards the top it begins to explode. There is a special glass room and a canopy at the top.

This is like a site in the round. They call it an office building, but it is not strictly so. It was very interesting because it meant doing architecture for the sake of architecture, whatever happened inside the building becoming really secondary. It is in a more residential area. The former building was demolished; we felt that if we were to take away

7. Azabu, Tokyo, 1987. Perspective view

8. Azabu, Tokyo, 1987. Model

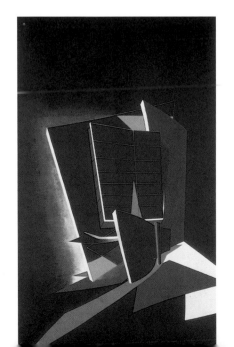
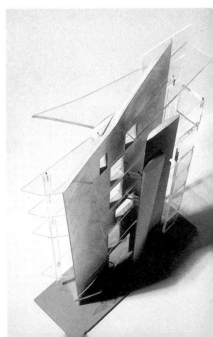

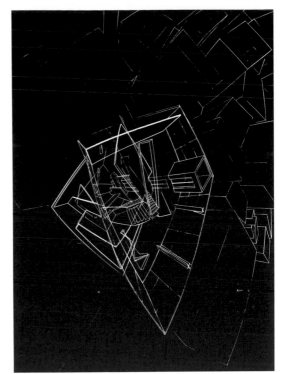

9. Tomigaya,
Tokyo, 1987. Office
building, model

10. Tomigaya,
Tokyo, 1987. Office
building, perspec-
tive from above

this building we would replace it with a vacuum or a void. There was to be no presence of architecture on this site.

The Tomigaya building is in three sections: one completely sunk into the ground, a central section which is open to the air and is part of Tokyo, and a room which becomes a pavilion. The three programs are almost flexible and are part of the city. The one below ground could become design studios or a gallery, the top room could be a recreation area, for example public lounges.

To manipulate the zone below ground we had to peel the floor away to let the light in; the staircase was inserted into this cut-out. There is a shallow room that takes you downstairs; we did computer animated images in order to show how we could use the space in terms of circulation. As you journey to the bottom of the building you land on a platform in the middle of the tall, enormous void. From there you can continue into the pit (figs. 9, 10).

All the volumes were originally connected by a pier, which eventually became a diagonal column that transfers below the ground.

When I went to Berlin one architect told me you had to make sure they don't treat your buildings like salami; they like to chop bits off, thinking it makes no difference to the overall plan. I thought this was

*11. Hafenstrasse,
Hamburg, 1989.
Model of
building I*

an interesting concept. So we used the salami technique in this Tokyo
project to establish the contours. We made templates of all the sections
so the concrete work would be absolutely perfect.

A year or so ago in Graz I met a Professor Kossak from Hamburg who
liked the Ku'damm project so much that he invited me to do two projects
in Hamburg, one of which starts from zero meters in width and is
twenty-two meters long. Both are on a very controversial street called
Hafenstrasse; of course I was completely ignorant of the riots caused by
the squatters on the site. There are fundamentally a series of gaps on the
skyline opposite the harbour. The intention was that they would be filled
in instead of demolishing the whole street. We had incredible problems
developing these two projects, because I could not do another Ku'damm.
I had two options: I could either do something completely different even
though we had established an almost perfect condition for ourselves, or
I could do a catalogue of as many Ku'damms as I could possibly make.
So the idea was that there is one building that is blown away by the wind
and the other one is slightly more in danger of being pushed, with no
definite physical form because it is compressed between two existing
buildings. We finally decided to make it like a normal slab that is pushed
sideways (fig. 11). It's a very simple building with open spaces for either
living or working. So we made a catalogue of the slabettes — it's not
a slab because it's too small.

The whole condition became like a graph that becomes highly
agitated as it hits the side. I required something other than a block.
Because the site has such a beautiful view, one needed an opening within
it in order to see the harbor more immediately.

So one site is the leaning slabette; I thought the other one should be like a bookcase with a stack of books (fig. 12). The problem was that the site was too small to show this intensity. It had to be clear that these are different buildings, and not just different walls that are sandwiched together. Each of the buildings would contain either studios, apartments, or offices. Because we had a client for the corner building but not for the middle one, the middle site remained a study. We used this middle building as a test as to how our ideas might be implemented.

The corner building leans over you as you stand on the street. What is interesting is that the floors, as they move back, remain almost identical; the only change that occurs is the location of the elevator. This is the twentieth version of the Ku'damm. Right at the top is a communal space, a sky lobby.

We showed our plans at an exhibition. We did a study of the two models as they leant backward and forward and one where the curtain wall was superimposed on the section to show the two together.

At the moment the different levels in the corner slabette are just linear spaces that are defined by a given program. They could be either undivided or split up if they are to be apartments. They could also be linked vertically.

So in the end we did the middle site as a test. We felt that we should test the idea again in the future if the opportunity arose. It could be applied to any waterfront condition where the skyline, the views, and the intensitiy of the program are critical.

In 1989 we had a very big project for a site in Düsseldorf. It has a multiple program because it is the first site to generate the harbor development in Düsseldorf. The central part of the project is for an advertising agency, the second deals with the landscape on the ground, and the third contains public facilities, film studios, design studios, offices, and a hotel. We had to consider whether the idea we had for Hamburg could be transported to Düsseldorf. It could work better because of the generosity of the site, a marina by the water. These are only very early studies as we won the competition only two months ago (figs. 13, 14). So there is a possibility that it will become reality. Compared to the work we have done in the last three years it's an excessively generous site. We felt that the site had to be seen as layers, as it dealt with so many layers of activities.

The site is divided into sections. The front part becomes part of the landscape and harbor and the second part becomes the series of public facilities that address the city and the site itself. The whole site is about two hundred meters long and fifty meters wide; there is a cut-out, a triangular piazza that slides into the site to become a private condition. In the park area there are public rooms carved out of the landscape.

There is a very long and linear building; it breaks at only one point. This is the headquarters of the agency, the intention being that the design disciplines within which the agency operates come together in a center. You enter a glass room as you walk along the street. You can also walk under a slab that acts as a canopy as it cantilevers over you. You see what seems like a blank wall — there are many surprises — and you also have very specific views over the water. The longer building could also have different layers like the Peak, consisting of hotel accommodation or offices. The only part that is separated is the agency; the idea is that it acts as a media center.

There is a piazza that slopes into the public zone. This contains offices, shops on the ground, an underground cinema, and studios. Each of the floors is adaptable to a different program; there could be a hotel on the seventh floor and offices on the second. It is a multilayered concept, an extension of the conditions of the city.

13. Düsseldorf, 1989. Building for multiple purposes

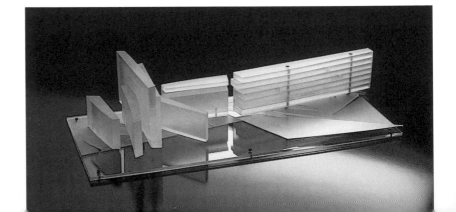

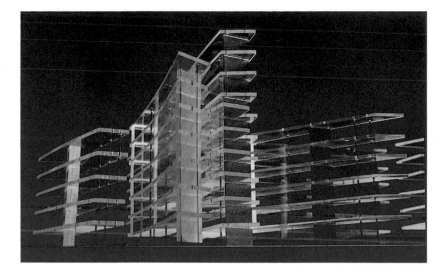

The long building is raised, providing a view of the harbor as one walks along the street.

What interested me was how one could create a condition where one can see one's neighbors in the same building but not get to them.

You enter a glass room and get onto a ramp as you go up the lobby. There is a separate space which is like a think-tank. The directors' rooms have no hierarchy because they all work on the same floor and come together in a rather amorphic meeting-space. The exchange of ideas occurs in this carved-out space. There are double-height rooms at the tip. They are not separated by their desires but by air. At some point in the building all these floors intermingle to become a normal building with continuous office floors. These floors are not partitioned but are divided by glass walls and air. It's a building under one umbrella.

The idea of these very intense spaces in the open came about with the studies we did for "folly," in Osaka. It is a very small project for a garden exposition in Osaka. It is a series of walls compressed together. What is interesting is the experience of moving through the spaces between the walls. The site is very strict — only seven and a half meters long — but they allowed us to make it a little longer. We didn't want to make it into an object which rested over the site, but a piece where one could move through uninterrrupted. All the walls, except for two concrete ones, are metallic. All the lighting comes from under the ground, so the whole thing looks as if it is floating.

The theme for a restaurant in Sapporo was "Ice and Fire." The ground floor restaurant is an iceberg; you enter this very cold room — all made of glass (fig. 15) — and the ice is then transformed into fire and melted away on the top floor bar (fig. 16). It is a rather ironic project. We designed sofas for the restaurant like snakes or eels floating in the box of ice. We painted the model of the building black, and Rossi's co-architect thought we painted the building black and he quite liked it. So the building became a black box — which might be a surprise to Aldo Rossi.

The "fire" zone upstairs, contains a low bar; you eat on couches. The architecture of the building is far removed from my sensibility — there is a central hall or dome. These are things I have never used before, and we originally wanted to explode the top. They said no, we couldn't do that; it was an Aldo Rossi building and we shouldn't mess around with it. What we did instead was to suspend the bar floor in the hall; this is the core of the project. The floor is glass so that you feel as though you are suspended over the floor below. The room above is predominantly very dark, except for the edges in color. The ground floor is in off-white colors and predominantly glass.

We had in mind the Japanese way of eating when we designed the very long, thin tables and low seats, even though this is an Italian restaurant.

My favorite project of recent years is a fire station for the Vitra furniture factory. They originally approached us to do a chair after seeing our furniture published. In time they asked me to design a fire station, because the factory is expanding and they have to accommodate for that. It is not just a fire station, it is also a fitness center. It involved designing the walls that surround the buildings of the site as well as a bicycle-shed and all the small elements that can be sprinkled on the factory.

15. Moonsoon Restaurant, Sapporo, 1990. 'Ice', downstairs restaurant

16. Moonsoon Restaurant, Sapporo, 1990. 'Fire', upstairs bar

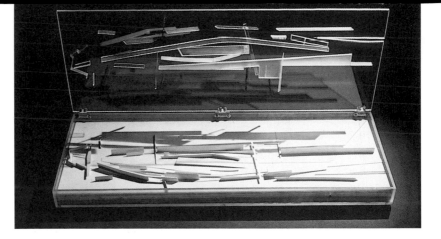

*17. Vitra Fire
Station, 1990.
Model*

I visited the site before the Frank Gehry building was erected. There
was a new building just being put up, so the site was made of enormous
pieces. It had no coherent structure; there was no way of tying it
together. I felt if we really followed the program strictly and put a fire-
station here and bicycle-shed there, it would be very difficult to make
sense of the whole thing. So we did a study of the landscape, as it was
imperative to me to really understand how to make a space out of this
no-man's no-space. I decided to concentrate all my energies on one zone.
We saw the space between the sheds as an open-air room and the
furniture for this room is the fire-station and all the pieces. The room
is the void and its reverse is solid. The intention is for them to build it
now so that it will seem like a solid, but when the second part of the
factory is built — which is on the other side — the central corridor
becomes a void. There is this play between all these things (fig. 17).

The connection between the inner streets is influenced by the line of
buildings. The open-air room or carved-out space appears as the factory
buildings take shape, and the walls of the buildings become like furniture.

The ground is manipulated by what one puts on it. In relation to the
overall landscape the surfaces become important. They could be gravel,
grass, concrete, in color or non-color.

They sent us a video of the choreography of the firemen. It was
exciting because they have to climb walls, pretending they have a fire,
and they have to cross a bridge over two buildings, almost like tightrope-
walkers. The room where the trucks are stored is seen as a very beautiful
room, but it could be just spatially very beautiful. The bicycle-shed could
be just a very simple roof resting in a cut-out section of land. There is
also the pedestrian connection between the new chair museum by Frank
Gehry and a new factory hall. The new route becomes an outside space
and has a lot of colors, surfaces and, coincidentally, a fire station.

And that's it. Thank you.

Daniel Libeskind

BETWEEN THE LINES

It seems to me that there is no way to camouflage the inability to speak about architecture coherently or from the beginning. The notion of an original point of departure, which presupposes a past, is in itself doubtful, because the past has never been experienced as being present. So I would rather skip the beginnings altogether and go straight to the middle, which in my case is the Berlin Museum with the Jewish Museum. But first I want to try to explain something about time — not only historical time, time in architecture, but also the time we are now living in. I came to the conclusion a while ago that when one is looking at time, looking at history, nothing seems to have taken place. One realizes that when one is looking at time, time is not playing along, time is not visible, so to speak, because one is looking for it. But then the minute you don't look for time you are transformed by it: suddenly it just happens overnight, so to speak, or between the drawings, or in between the works, that one has been completely transformed.

Thus, to speak about architecture (or to speak about Berlin and about the contemporary situation) is to speak about the paradigm of the irrational. In my view, the best works of the contemporary spirit come from the irrational, while what prevails in the world, what dominates and often kills, does so always in the name of Reason. The irrational as a nonbeginning of this project was my starting point. Berlin is not only a physical place, but also something in the mind, something belonging to a past which never was present. A spiritual reality that makes itself immediately comprehensible to everyone in the world. We all know John F. Kennedy's statement "I am a Berliner." but it occurs to me that not only is everyone a Berliner, but after the tragic and disastrous consequences of the Holocaust and its impact on Modernity everyone is also a survivor. Everyone who witnessed these ultimate events is also a survivor, so one cannot die the death of a victim anymore.

The rabbis and the commentaries on the Talmud sometimes say that God created the world out of nothing, a something out of nothing, and

1. Interior of museum,
fragments and the void

that it is the responsibility of the faithful to try to extract from this something the creative nothingness from which it came. Now this obviously involves one in something irrational from the very beginning, because I can't tell you how 'nothing' started. But I can tell you the three elements that interested me about the project of the Berlin Museum with the Jewish Museum.

I started by trying to plot a hexagonal figure, I don't know why. In a way it sounds very kitsch, the star of David, it's such a cliché. Around the site on Lindenstrasse there lived so many famous Germans, and many famous Jews. Jews, Germans, all Berliners, people who formed the culture we know as "Berlin." I went about trying to find out the addresses of Berliners like Kleist, Heine, and Rahel Varnhagen, but also of more contemporary Berliners like Schoenberg, Paul Celan, Walter Benjamin. Of course, where they lived isn't significant for the pattern of the city, it's not important where those anonymous addresses were, but nevertheless I found them. I then tried to make a connection between those who were the carriers of the spiritual entity of Berlin as an emblem, and I ended up with a kind of distorted hexagonal set of lines. It was a framework: I did not want to begin with a grid, or with a square or a module, but I had to start somewhere in the nowhere. This rather irrational set of lines forms a nexus that links up certain anonymous places in Berlin, both East and West. But it is also a series of connections between unreal places and real people. That's one dimension, let's call it the architectonic dimension, the irrational invisible matrix, of the project.

2. Signature matrix

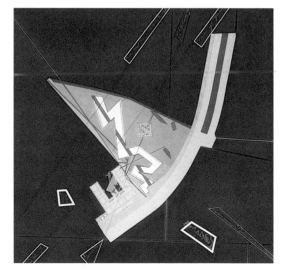

The second dimension of the project is a musical dimension. I have long been fascinated by Schoenberg's unfinished opera *Moses and Aaron*. What now interested me about the work was not only that it had twelve letters in the title (*Moses and Aron*) and all its other serial aspects, but the fact that Schoenberg started it in Berlin, but could not finish it. Only acts I and II were composed. It is not only that he had no inspiration, so to speak, to complete act III, but the whole musical structure had ground to a halt, erasing the possibility of continuing in the operatic mode. It intrigued me that such a genius, an incredible intellect and a great composer, was unable to complete act III. So I got out my records and started reading the libretto. Then I became aware that the opera really deals with the Berlin Museum. It was written a long time before, but, as I said, time does not work that way. It is a dialogue between Aaron and Moses, Aaron being the mouthpiece of the people of Israel, and Moses the one who understands that there is nothing to show the people. Aaron wants to communicate to the people, lead them into the promised land, and Moses is unable to convey the revelation of God through any image, including the musical image in Schoenberg's case. The discussion between Aaron and Moses ends up with Aaron slowly exiting in the background, and then the chorus sings "Almighty, Thou art stronger than Egyptian gods are!" and then everybody leaves and Moses is left alone to sing the words: Inconceivable God! Inexpressible, many-sided idea, will You let it be so explained? Shall Aaron, my mouth, fashion this image? Then I have fashioned an image too, false, as an image must be. Thus am I defeated! Thus, all was but madness that I believed before, and can and must not be given voice." All this is sung, but the last line, "O word, thou word, that I lack!" is not sung any more, it's just spoken. At the end of the opera you can understand the word because there is no music: the word, so to speak, has been isolated and given a completely nonmusical expression. That's the end of the opera as Schoenberg composed it.

So that is the second dimension of the project. The first is the nexus of lines connecting invisibles that are not patterned on the cityscape, the second is the unfinished act III of Schoenberg's opera, and the third is a book, let's call it the textual dimension. For this I got myself two volumes. I wrote to the Federal Information Office in Bonn and asked if they had any book that contained the names of all the Jewish people who were deported from Berlin. They did indeed have such a list, and it came to me in the mail. It's an incredible two-volume set, like a giant, black telephone-book, with nothing in it but names in alphabetical order, an amazing publication. Just names, dates of birth and dates of deportation and places in different parts of Europe where millions of Jews were exterminated by Germans. And I looked for the names of Berliners, of course, since this was a Berlin project, a Berlin museum. That was the third dimension.

I also thought that the museum for such a place as Berlin should not be only for the citizens of the present, but should be accessible, let's say imaginatively or metaphysically, to citizens of the past and of the future, a place for all citizens of Berlin to confirm their common heritage. Since they are all Berliners, were Berliners, and will be Berliners, they should also find in it a shared hope, which is something created in individual desire. To this end I saw that the museum form needed to be rethought, in order to discourage the passivity of the public in the museum. I thought that a museum should not simulate a culture, but should

4. Site

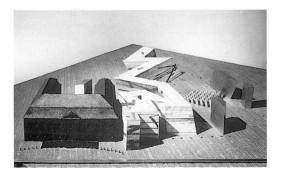

5. *View from Lindenstrasse*

6. *View from the east*

distance or involve the public, in order to make them decide how, where and what to do in a museum whose particular function is the history of the city, and of an emblem. Thus, the extension to the Berlin Museum, with its special function of housing the Jewish Museum, is an attempt to give voice to a common fate, common to Jews, to non-Jews, to Berliners, to non-Berliners, to those who live abroad and those who live at home, those in exile, and those in the wilderness. And this fate is shared between being and what is completely other than being. So it's not only about space, not only an existential continuum, but also something completely other than text, completely other than construction, completely other than knowledge. It's not only about Existence but also about Inexistence. It seems to me that modern philosophy is really not an existential philosophy at all, although it starts with existential philosophy and continues towards what seems to be modeled after a philosophy of something, it finally disappears and is reduced to a philosophy of exile, a philosophy of deprivation. You can say it is "inexistential" philosophy, and this perhaps is also one of the definitions of Modernism and Postmodernism.

In any case, the museum should serve not only to inspire poetry, music and drama, but should give a home to the ordered — disordered, the welcome — unwelcome, the chosen — not chosen, the helpful — unhelped, the vocal which is silent. And so it should, at least in my program, go across these divisions. It should become a spiritual site, not only an architectural and urban piece of real estate. It should at least have in it the precariousness of Berlin's destiny, which it should mirror, fracture, and at the same time transgress. The past fatality of the German-Jewish cultural symbiosis is being reenacted now, but in the realm of that which cannot be seen. There is today no Jewish presence in Berlin as there was in the twenties and thirties and back in the eighteenth and nineteenth centuries, but in a way it is still there, except that it is not something one can see. And it is this "not seeing-not seen" aspect that should be brought to visibility, in order to give rise to a hope and to a sharing of an inner vision. The project seeks to reconnect this trace of history to Berlin and Berlin to its own eradicated history, which should not be camouflaged, disowned or forgotten. I sought to reopen the meaning which seems to be only implicit in Berlin and to make it visible, to make it apparent, not to try to hide it or to disown it. So I took the great figures in the drama — or rather, the great figures in the drama of Berlin took me. Those who acted as the bearers of the once imminent hope and the bearers of a great anguish, of a great pathos: these I tried to graft into the building and the site.

The new extension is conceived as an emblem where the not visible has made itself apparent as a void, an invisible. The idea is very simple: to build the museum around a void that runs through it, a void that is to be experienced by the public. Physically, very little remains of the Jewish presence in Berlin — small things, documents, archive materials, evocative of an absence rather than a presence. I thought therefore that this "void" that runs centrally through the contemporary culture of Berlin should be made visible, accessible. It should become the structural feature that is crystallized in this particular space of the city and laid bare in an architecture in which the unnamed remains because the names keep still. The existing building, and it is actually one of the oldest Baroque buildings in the center of Berlin, should be tied in depth to this new building, but with no apparent connection on the outside. The extension has no apparent connection to the existing building of the Berlin Museum. It has an underground connection to it, in order to preserve the contradictory autonomy of the buildings on the surface, while binding them even more in depth. So the underground connection is the archival element of the Jewish Museum; when you come out of

7. View from the southwest

it you come into the Void, which is an organizational and a structural element of the Berlin Museum as well as of the Jewish Museum. Under, above, and on the ground. Like Berlin and its Jews, it is a common burden, an insupportable burden. There is nothing to support it. It is immeasurable, unsharable. It is outlined in exchanges between two architectures and forms that are not reciprocal, because they cannot be exchanged for each other.

The urban, architectural, and functional paradox of what has been closed and opened, what is stable and what is added, what is Baroque and what is Modern, what is a museum and what is amusement, is no longer reconcilable, in my view, through a theory, a theoretical construction, a theoretical utopia. It can no longer presuppose the fictitious stability of institutions such as museums, or indeed of the state, of power, of organization. Rather, the paradox between these dichotomies presupposes the Unchanging.

I called this talk "Between the Lines," but it's really between two lines of thought: one is a straight line, but broken into fragments; the other is tortuous and complex, but continuing indefinitely. These are the two lines of contemporary dichotomy, the lines which create the rift between faith and action, between political belief and architectural response. These lines develop themselves, because they have a logic. They also fall apart: you can't keep them together, because they become completely disengaged, there's no way to keep them mutually intertwined. Therefore, the lines show themselves as separated, so that the void, which has been centrally running through what is continuous, materializes itself outside as what has been ruined, or rather as the remnant or residue of independent structure. I call this the "voided void," a void which has itself been voided, a deconstruction which has itself been deconstructed. Fragmentation and displacement mark the coherence of the ensemble in this type of operation, because the thing has come undone in order to become accessible, both functionally and intellectually.

I believe that the last words, the inaudible music, the inadequate ideology, the mad science have become undone in order to be understood by us, in order to become intellectually and spiritually comprehensible. These torn pieces of history never pre-existed as a whole, neither in the ideal Berlin nor in the real one. Nor do I believe that they can be put together again, in some hypothetical future. First of all, it's not true that Berlin ever was the way one inherited it through the Goethe myth, the Schinkel myth, the myth of the twenties — it never was like that in the first place. That illusion is now the spacing, or the distance brought about by history itself, which can only be experienced as an absence, or as the time-fulfillment of what was no longer there.

On the other hand, time is fulfilled for those things which are not here any more, both on the urban level and on the level of the collection and the program of the museum. The absolute event of history is the Holocaust and the incineration of the avantgarde of humanity in its own history. Should we not think of Nagasaki and Hiroshima in the light of this avantgardeness in which humanity and history seem to be coincident? This event of history, with its concentration-camps and annihilation, is, I believe, the burnout of meaningful development of the city of Berlin, and of humanity. It's not only on the physical level that I would

9. Inner structure

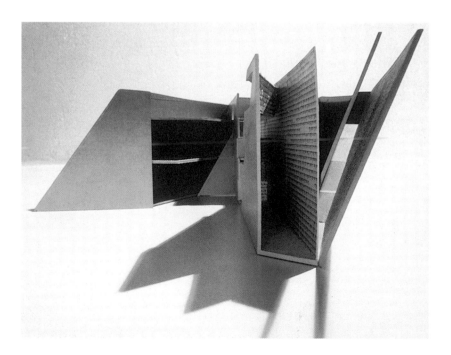

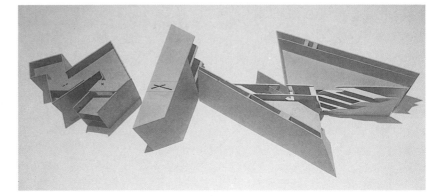

like to demonstrate that there is a possibility, but also on other levels; because absence shatters each place while bestowing a gift of that which no architecture can give — a gift given by no one, for no one; the preservation of the sacrifice, the offering, which guards over future meaning. That's what architecture, the arts and the sciences are vested with: the responsibility of a nightwatch over meaning which is not there and over meaning which might have, nobody knows, been given. So out of the disaster, out of history, rises what is not historical. And out of what is terribly remote, there comes the intimate whisper.

Thom Mayne

CONNECTED ISOLATION

Ladies and Gentlemen, Friends of Architecture:

To talk about architecture today, given our global context, would be difficult without establishing some general parameters of understanding. Hence the obligation I feel this evening to introduce myself and to attempt to define the issues that are central to our work.

I was educated in the late sixties when most schools of architecture in the United States were circumscribed by the tenets of Utopian Determinism and a somewhat dogmatic, Eurocentric modernism. There was a tremendous energy propelling us into the future (we were all planning for *the future*) with holistic visions and a rationale of analysis and synthesis. The focus was on infrastructures with their emphasis on program, change and flexibility, and the environment. The objective was a generic, neutral architecture resulting in a pure manifestation of information. Architecture was a social art, produced collectively. There was an implicit antagonism toward the private or the personal. It was, of course, a time of great social and political activity; there was great optimism regarding the collective aspirations of an otherwise pragmatic society rooted in concepts of the autonomy of the individual, with their attendant definitions of freedom.

Today, it is impossible to assess a common system of values within our pluralistic world, where reality is chaotic, unpredictable, and hence ultimately unknowable. Hazard has become the principle by which we operate, increasingly influenced by the mass media and by the collective impact of decisions which have been decentralized through our economic and political institutions. The tendency is to perpetuate values designed to optimize the normative and the consumptive aspects of a society that serves the needs of a middle class in its search for self-determination. One of the central themes of architecture today is the question of whether one can act *independently* from the psychological and social forces inherent within this environment, forces which erode the autonomy, the self-awareness, even the sanity of the individual.

1. Kate Mantilini Restaurant.
Orrery under construction, 1986

One of the refuges available to us in this circumstance is the world of intimate life — that secret, precious sphere which is the basis for originality and can be utilized as the generative source for observing and investigating human existence. We live this life circumstantially, and understand it through our own capacities — it is ours, it is personal. It offers us different possibilities for action. Life is a permanent crossroads and a constant perplexity. José Ortega y Gasset talks of "the essence of man as purely and simply danger. Man always travels among precipices and, whether he will or not, his truest obligation is to stay in balance."

Given this situation, I believe we are now obliged to ask ourselves what validity there is in the definition of architecture as a social art. I believe that we must confront ourselves and our perception of the world in its complexity. This complexity is fostered by the density and sheer magnitude of information and the attendant specialization, which diminishes our ability to understand phenomena coherently. The acceleration of the rate of change (of time itself) in the twentieth century further complicates this situation by placing our lives in a milieu of continuous flux. So much of 'architecture' today attempts to resist this situation by asserting some notion of a more comfortable and static past (Prince Charles comes to mind). One is meant to feel safe and on familiar ground upon experiencing it. But this comfort ignores our future and our responsibility to address the issues of our time. We have no choice but to acknowledge the world's complexity and the very conditions that define our *contemporary* society.

ON CONTEXT

Los Angeles is in many ways prototypical of the contemporary metropolis. No longer is it possible to conceive of an impregnable city. There is no comprehension of the whole, there are no clear boundaries, only layers of mostly unperceivable infrastructure, which appear as non sequiturs. Working within this context obligates us to ask questions fundamental to the broader urban, collective aspirations of our work. The burden of this situation is inescapable, since its source lies not primarily within the discipline, but in the program of society. We have no choice but to accept it, to absorb it, and ultimately to devise strategies in our art to encourage a symbiosis between our work and our community.

There are other more conceptual forms of context which interest us. There is a still form from Man Ray's Dada film *Return to Reason*. It is the torso of Kiki de Montparnasse streaked with light and shadow. A decisive step was taken here, announcing the elaboration of a radically new conception of the world and of matter. There is a sense of *juxta-*

position, two dynamic bodies connected by light (energy) through a membrane. Both of these images are about the status of the individual within a relational framework and focus on the *interconnectedness* of things.

Every design initiative, on whatever scale, is a fragment embedded in a larger context and is understood through this association. In our early work — the freestanding additions in Venice, California, for example — we were interested in the relationship of "*connection*" and "*autonomy*." The 2-4-6-8 Project (fig. 2) was the beginning of a series of quasi-vernacular buildings that utilized interpretations of their found environments as instigators of an architectural language. The departure point was a platonic cube, the basis for the ideal/contingent dialogue. The Sedlak project reiterates most of these interests but utilizes an operational strategy which erodes the parts and attempts to become more hybrid in nature. Both projects are interested in the '*monument-ness*' endemic to architecture and in their roles as animators of human existence and of our need to remember.

The Lawrence residence juxtaposes or collides two building types which aim to produce what we thought of as a new *sub*-urban prototype. We sought to synthesize the two prevalent building types characteristic of Venice, a small California coastal town. We were most interested in the physiognomic characteristics of their types and the transmittal of information through the architectural language, each appropriating the characteristics normative to its type. While the project was being realized, it became increasingly apparent that there was a problem in the

2. 2-4-6-8 House. Exterior, 1978 – 80

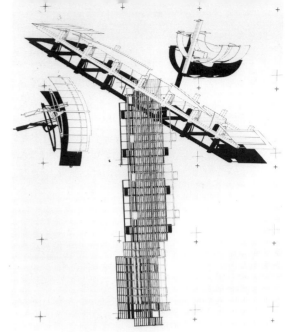

3. *Venice III*
(Bergren
Residence).
Exterior, 1982 – 84

4. *Leon Max*
Showroom.
Presentation
drawing: "Four
free-standing
objects, suggestive
of the machinery
of the production
process, engaged in
a dialogue with
the pre-existing
conditions of the
space formed by
the grid of the
concrete columns."
1988

literal manner in which we interpreted these models. The synthesis lacked the tension we were seeking as the manifestation of the inter-action.

The Venice III freestanding studio addition (fig. 3) allowed us to continue our exploration which started with the first two Venice houses and, in particular, responded to our critique of the last project. Here, I think we were able to translate our ideas into a more abstracted frame-work — an architecture, *thickly described*, that attempts to reflect the rich and dense textures of a heterogenous society. It is simultaneously "a part" of its context and also isolated, critical, mistrustful of the world as it exists. Deformations of an idealized geometry instil in it the charac-teristics of a hazardous and imperfect world. We were now becoming more interested in articulating the *differences* and *contradictions* found in the diversity of our culture.

Within the context of an internal site such as the Leon Max industrial building in downtown L.A., objects (suggestive of machinery and the *process of production*) exemplify the various functions that are part of this showroom (fig. 4). Referring to the dynamic aspects of the *making pro-cess*, they establish a dialogue with the more permanent architecture of the existing building. One's understanding of these architectural objects in relation to site (building) includes other objects (clothing) within the modular units which are perceived through the translucency of the screen as color (which changes seasonally).

Increasing amounts of our work in Los Angeles are interventions in existing buildings. Our interest in these projects continues our investigations into connection and confrontation, with its passive and active associations. The work speaks of its place *and* reshapes it. This particular site offered us the opportunity to pursue our interests in creating public spaces that are intentionally ambiguous in their definition and hence become exercises in discussing boundaries and edges.

In the Kate Mantilini orrery (fig. 1) we used the oculus (an internal orreum) as the foundation or site for an architectural construction that is an instrument of observation and description, a kind of architectural voyeur. The emphasis is not on the oculus as the event placing light within this space, but on its use as identifying a particular site for this mechanism. Fragments of the project compose this structure, which is in the process of making or recording the larger work. The orrery is about the self-reflecting, self-referential nature of architecture. It is a mirror; the real subject is the spectator. The simplicity of the bounding wall, alive with natural light (light is the connector), aspires to recall the generic nature of a wall throughout time and serves as a backdrop and counterpoint for the whole entity.

There are some circumstances in which the *context is the project*. The problem we faced with the Comprehensive Cancer Center was in developing a design strategy which could clarify and organize a difficult subterranean site impacted between three existing buildings. A framework of geometries, both similar and diverse in character, establish a language of distinct autonomous spaces. It is through the perception and understanding of these discrete units and their particular architectural properties that one becomes oriented. The development of the sectional aspect of this building was an outgrowth of the connection of the new structure (with its light gathering, sky-oriented potentialities) to the existing hospital space. The two major spaces of the building, the reception area and the chemotherapy atrium, were conceived as a datum for the total scheme and reflect the complex's relationship to the ground and the sky. The planes of the roof oscillate between transparency and translucency, producing spaces that are understood to be both exterior and interior in nature (fig. 5). Through the development of an architectural language of light, volume, scale, depth and increment, the departments within this 55,000 square foot complex reinterpret the basic themes of these two spaces.

The waiting room of the CCC (fig. 6) serves as a place for a childrens' 'play' structure; it is a more conceptual space dealing with the building's own construction using fragments (real or imagined) of man-made and natural elements. The whole enterprise seeks to communicate a feeling of connection with the outside world. It is through one's connection with natural forces that one might make contact with one's inner, more

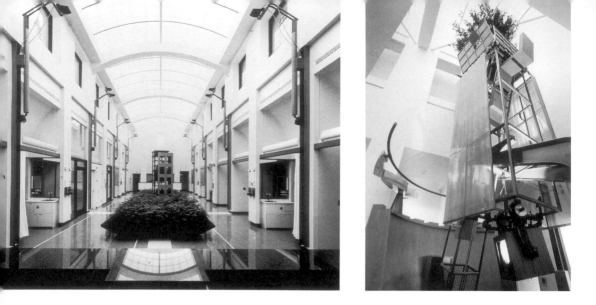

contemplative nature. The aspiration is to an architecture that will occupy the mind, affect the spirit, and act as a foil to the patient's current circumstance by removing him or her from self-occupation.

All these projects are concerned with the occupation and meaning of their sites and the ability to utilize their idiosyncratic characteristics to form a basis for the work's more autonomous aspects. In the end it is this middle territory between connection and confrontation that most challenges us: a work which can be about interaction *and* isolation.

ON PROCESS AND MAKING

A second broad area of continuity within our explorations is based on the ideas of conceptualization and construction. Thinking leads to action. We think to resolve problems which require action. Conceptualizing and making are the terms in architecture. The work itself must finally signify its meaning and its intentions. It must have the capability to translate ideas into the concrete. The conceptual ideas are paralleled by an interest in the process of construction and the expressive capacity of the materials of the built object. The drawings for the 2-4-6-8 house replaced the traditional working documents. They are more in keeping with our interest in the complexity behind an apparent simplicity. There is a concern here for the expression of a series of articulated parts constructing a cohesive whole. Technology is at the *service* of the work. The processes of conceptualization and construction are fundamental to our work. The value and presence of material, the recall of construction and making, and our attempts to document and describe the forces inherent in a project are our primary concerns.

It is the nature of architecture to manifest presence, to be the agent of reality — bricks and mortar, shelter and function. We are interested in the relationship of concepts and their manifestation in a material presence. An authenticity lies within this presence. Much of our perception and understanding of architecture exists through the sensuality of its own matter. Pleasure and beauty live in this sensuality. Architecture gives this reality an imaginary coherence that makes reality appear natural and eternal.

One of the powers of architecture is its nondependence on realization. Drawings can dismantle or disregard material and weight, providing insight into the unattainable. They are also so much more private — you can possess them, inhabit them, in a manner so different from the work. Drawings can represent a resistance to our dualistic tendencies, integrating intuition and rationality.

We continue to construct fragments or armatures of projects that are linked by a common purpose or intention (fig. 7). This is a method which leads us to seeing a single work as a collection of diverse self-generated autonomous centers. Each represents a partial or fragmentary vision of reality; the fragment is understood as *unfinished* with an implicit connotation of the future (or the potential for a future).

Ideas concerning transparency are one of the most relevant features of our time. This photogram, understood as a diagrammatic record of the motion of light translated into black, white, and gray values, can lead to a grasp of new types of spatial relationships and spatial rendering. It provides simultaneous knowledge of the inside and of the outside ... the

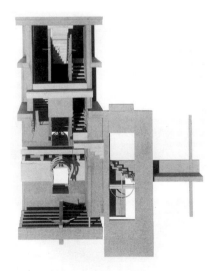

7. *Was House.*
Model fragment,
1988

8. Politix (retail store), Portland. Space modulator, 1990

view of an opaque solid, its outline, but also its inner structure. The 4th generation video image of a table I designed is about potential. It records change and movement and the deception of appearance — *what we don't see.*

This drodel (half drawing — half model, fig. 8) intensifies the atmospheric quality of the space while dematerializing the manner in which space is formed and perceived. It explores simultaneous interior/exterior viewpoints of a single building on 68 plates of glass.

The use of models and drawings as working tools can describe both the conceptual forces that shape the work and the processes it undergoes. In this case both drawing and model (one simulated, one realized) magnify irregularity, fluctuation, and instability.

Our work with small scale objects contributes ideas to the architectural projects, particularly at a secondary or tertiary level. Most of these objects use the human figure (or animal anatomy — 98% of our genes are shared with chimps) as a point of reference and are seen as extensions of the body. They are vaguely prosthetic or symbiotic, all share physiognomic qualities with animals, such as the Barking Dog Lamp, which is acutally a guard lamp. Sisyphus condemned to perpetual repetition. Sensors responding to movement and sound, activate tongue and jaw. The canister (body) contains the light (energy).

The Nee Chair, part normative chair and part found object, responds to weight. Our work on these objects closes the time lag between idea and manifestation; it has forced us to better understand and to expand our knowledge of the processes inherent in the making. It is, at this level, about architecture.

TOWARDS AN ARCHITECTURE OF CONNECTED ISOLATION

Our interest in appropriating site situations as instigators of the formal direction of the work is paralleled by an interest in an interior architecture which is detached and isolated from its environment and offers a counterpoint to the contingencies of the city. The more disciplined internal order of the Venice studio project was an outgrowth of the spatial armature within the Lawrence residence.

The Venice III studio (see fig. 2), the last of our "buildings that scare little children" series, pursues a strategy that juxtaposes a secluded and idealized interior with an exterior, reflecting the contradictions rooted in the diverse characteristics of the site condition. Three repetitive *light/room* increments form the core of the work, establishing the predominance of these private spaces and their earth-sky connections.

For me, natural light is the most complex and meaningful light, because it is dynamic — it is one of the only grounds of common agreement for man — it puts us in touch with the rhythms of our own body. Each of these platonic volumes develops specific architectural qualities as it accommodates function. The two major interior spaces are empty — open to the light. They challenge the notion of a fixed center.

The connection or opening to the sky has been utilized in much of our work to create and clarify internal structure and the *horizonless* nature of the site. The various types of openings describe the intentions of the spaces which are simultaneously connecting to and detaching from the existing building. The light flooding this space helps to isolate or detach the architecture that makes it. A relatively complex space is made still more dynamic through its interaction with the sun.

Of our early work, the Sixth Street (fig. 9) project best synthesizes our interests. A single interior volume is the consequence of an implosion of its peripheral bounding surfaces (deep and volumetric), which are formed in response to their particular site circumstance (N.E.S.W.). Our constituent concerns for structure, use, durability, and order are here exemplified. We're interested in the coexistence of fragments leading to an unexpected harmony in an architecture which allows one to be at home in the world without feeling complacent about it. We're still pursuing the tensions and contradictions inherent in the strategy.

At some point we began working on various machine-like objects. This was an idea derived from our interest in the deterioration of

9. Sixth Street House. Line drawing, 1988

10. Higashi Azabu Tower, Tokyo. Model, 1988

materials. The elements were conceived as fragments of ruins — in themselves a reflection of the vanity of architecture and the power of nature. Robert Smithson talks about decay as implicit in all growth, in which the future is the past in reverse. In this inverted process, buildings don't fall into ruin after they are built, but rather rise into ruin before they are built. It is a method to free us of time. There is an aspect of this idea which corresponds to the notion of value ... the value which in our society equates the preciousness of materials with the importance of an architecture. This building negates the equation by its use of exhausted or discarded materials — flotsam and jetsam.

As in all of our projects, there is a correlation between the formal conceptual order and use. The various pieces have various functions: stairs, wall fragments, shower assemblies, etc. The ten elements are somewhat hierarchical, in that the most formally dominant pieces function in a wide range of disparate uses.

The urban intentions that were so much a part of the residential projects became the foundation for the larger scale work. Like its predecessors, the Higashi Azabu Building (fig. 10) is informed by the city but aspires to change it, attempting to establish a framework to accentuate the tension between the urban body as a whole and its constituent parts.

Located on a narrow, corner site in the center of Tokyo, the project comprises a restaurant, gallery, and general offices. The restaurant occupies the subterranean level visible from the two major streets and is accessed through a stair at the interior property line. The gallery is located on the street level and is made up of a two-level high space which is sky-lit and contains a mezzanine for ancillary gallery functions. The remaining six floors are general office space, culminating in a glass penthouse.

The slenderness of the building is exaggerated through a series of thick planes. The perception of the resultant configuration is one of a series of ambiguous endings or boundaries to the connecting urban block and forms the basis of the functional organization. A shear in the cross-section of the building, which reiterates the longitudinal layer, produces the space for entry and organizes the vertical movement systems to their associated volumes.

Our competition submission for the library addition at the Amerika Gedenkbibliothek was conceived as part of an urban ensemble in accordance with the site's historical and continuing importance in Berlin. The intent of our proposal is to develop a library that is both object and contextual ground (fig. 11) The positioning of the new complex is intended to simultaneously reinforce and reinterpret the original architectural strategy. Our project proposes a strategy of accretion, allowing for a multiple number of readings of the final complex.

The concept generates outward from a core to the specificity and idiosyncrasy of site and program. The core has two parts: a solid, the main public reading room and the stacks, and a void, which is the entry courtyard responding to the "force" of the Friedrichstrasse axis, both

11. Amerika
Gedenkbibiliothek.
Model, 1988

*12. Crawford
Residence. Model,
plan view,
1988—90*

maintaining and denying its historic continuity. In our solution we strove to overcome the isolation of the various parts and to engender between them a palpable sense of interdependence and interaction, yet not suppressing the identity of their separate roles. There is a direct relationship between the urban intentions and the internal functioning of the new complex. The proposed addition will be an architecture which will enhance one's comprehension of location and choice of movement. The new pedestrian circulation system is linear and perpendicular to the Friedrichstrasse axis. It is predicated on one's perception of the court's formal termination.

The existing park is augmented by pieces of old and new: historical tracers and the new project. The major organizing gesture is an arcade of trees (borrowing and reiterating the formal idea of the original library) to produce definition and put focus on the physical and social relationship of the Church. The trees extend the geometry of the children's library (which is literally *in* the park). Paths define past urban block configurations while fragments of the new building make places; both gestures are intended to make the park transitional or interstitial.

DIFFERENTIAL REPETITION

With the commission for the Crawford Project we proceeded with our interests in the development of an architecture corresponding to a site strategy within a rural context. The project interrelates three organizing systems which describe the site at three ranges of scale. The first, with its implication for a global connection, is the Cardinal grid. The second is a series of linear progressions perpendicular to the axis of the major view orientation, responding to a localized site condition. The core of this system emanates form a series of repetitive light monitors, each encompassing an obelisk-like element. The third system is based on fragments of a circular wall which form idealized notions of the private boundary (fig. 12).

The Crawford residence is derived from markings on the ground which describe rhythm and measurement. The exactitude of mathematics is relativized by the imprecision of human nature. The more systematic elements of the project provide a background for accidents and the exploitation of chance. There is a relationship between the insistence of repetition and the notion of simultaneous grasp, vision in motion. A series of isolated phenomena are integrated into a coherent whole. Time and movement become the subject of visual analysis. The repetitive system refers to this kind of coherency. The use of multiple objects places value on the in-between.

The project is engaged in a series of additive or subtractive gestures of the ground. Rooms (exterior) provide transition and connection to the larger site, breaking down *boundaries* of natural and man-made. The entry point documents one of the sites centers and makes the visual connection to the ocean approximately one half mile away. We want to exploit the broader assets of the site.

Our ongoing conversation about the environment is grounded in the ancient dichotomy of man versus nature. So far, society has sought to resolve the argument through a series of truces, either sequestering large tracts of wilderness in a state of imagined innocence, or limiting the ways in which man can domesticate nature's imagined savagery. We must begin to talk about man and nature, not man *versus* nature.

With our Chiba, Japan project we pursued many ideas from the Crawford project within a more abstract language and on an increased scale, attempting to resolve this traditional conflict through integration.

It is the site specific strategy that underscores the power of architectural form to claim and transform space. Architecture and landscape are inextricably fused.

The proposal utilizes a strategy of repetition as part of the larger issue of synthesizing man and nature. Repetition implies a denial of the insistence of the object. The emphasis is now on the space in-between. To string elements together without emphasis on logical termination defeats the idea of a fixed center or focus, further breaking down notions of the object (fig. 13).

The volumes of space and light are the departure point for an extroverted, outward thrusting scheme in the Crawford residence. In the

Chiba project these spacial increments are the result of an implosion of the two exterior site engulfing walls. They also address a subterranean condition which further exploits both the ground-sky interface and the private nature of the interior spaces. This monitor is the increment and building block of the project. The light rooms are now much larger in scale. Each room is simultaneously the same and specific to its immediate location. The intent is to use the system of light apertures as a background and unifying framework for a highly differentiated set of localized conditions (fig. 14). There is a tension set up between repetition and these idiosyncratic places.

SYSTEMS AND THE IDIOSYNCRATIC

The Vienna Expo project represents a synthesis of our work that attempts to integrate architecture and landscape through our investigations utilizing interacting organizational systems. We were particularly interested in the differentiation of the site conditions as manifested in late twentieth-century Vienna. The site is the result of temporal accumulations of space and objects, a process in which we now have the opportunity to participate. This found condition was the starting point for a project that rejects the classification of the city in terms of differentiated generic functions — living, working, recreation, transportation — with rigid zoning concepts. It challenges the notion that every program type has a one-to-one equivalent form type.

The new plan is made up of three major elements: a matt (ground) building, a series of autonomous structures, and various pieces of support and transportation infrastructure.

13. Golf Club at Chiba Prefecture. Model, 1988 — present

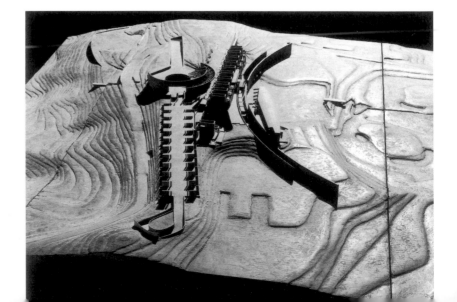

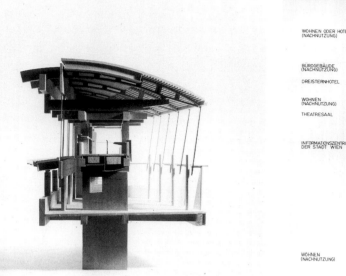

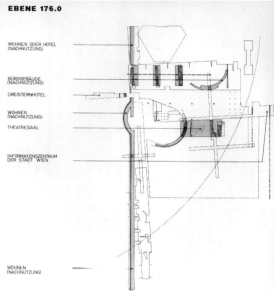

WOHNEN ODER HOTEL
(NACHNUTZUNG)

BÜROGEBÄUDE
(NACHNUTZUNG)

DREISTERNHOTEL

WOHNEN
(NACHNUTZUNG)

THEATRESAAL

INFORMATIONSZENTRUM
DER STADT WIEN

WOHNEN
(NACHNUTZUNG)

14. Golf Club at Chiba Prefecture. Model, section through restaurant, 1988 – present

15. Vienna Expo '95. Model, 1990

The matt element is the "container" defining the limits of our proposal. It is a type of 3D abstract map, which documents the various strata of information specific and idiosyncratic to the site and attempts to enhance its density. The contained curved surface, with its irregular periphery is itself a fragment, a fragment within a greater fragmentation, broken away from the whole, which is simultaneously part of its context (fig. 15). The surface of this structure forms a large scale public space connecting the bank of the Danube with the interior of the site (U.N. City). The manipulation of this site envelope produces a series of controlled accidents resulting in fissures or "places-in-between" where more defined public activity occurs. The scheme uses a series of juxtaposed or transparent orders as a background and unifying framework for a highly differentiated set of specific activities within the matt structure. This fabric contains a variety of functions including housing, commercial and institutional uses.

The object structures derive from an extension of the system interactions that formed the matt. These isolated buildings take on more normative associations and hierarchical roles in their placement. The interrelationship of free-standing buildings and ground buildings has allowed us to perceptually de-scale the total complex and produce a series of public spaces that reinforce a pedestrian scale.

The planning concept represents a flexible strategy for the future Expo '95, adaptable to a multiplicity of final programmatic configurations (fig. 16). The idea condenses the built aspects of the Expo phase onto the confines of the landscaped matt and the bridge (a linear cultural cross-section), which allows for the continuation of recreational uses of the island and the bank of the Danube. The general concept for the scheme considers the infrastructure of Expo '95 to be the departure point and core for a new district. Three primary categories of transformation are planned to occur in the second phase: elements which remain with only minor alterations (parking, exhibit space, the theaters, existing service, and commercial areas, new transport pieces, and the hotel complex); program elements that change from Expo use to post-Expo activities (some commercial, entertainment, and service space within the infrastructure); new elements that transform the site into its post-Expo condition (offices, additional commercial space, and housing).

The Vienna project in the end is about mathematical and geometric descriptions of natural and manmade events. There is no equilibrium, the systems have been submerged, allowing for the expression of a series of highly differentiated isolated structures. Man has been conquered by his circumstances.

CONCLUSION

16. Vienna Expo '95.
Photostat, plan, 1990

In this brief discussion of our work, I have sought to acquaint you as best I could with my concerns and intentions as an architect. I believe that

architecture cannot escape an active engagement in the issues and conditions of our contemporary society. We cannot stand apart from or above these issues, be they social, ethical, cultural, technical or ecological, because it is only by facing them that we may find a significant subject for our art. But having acknowledged this, it is equally clear that we must not confuse the subject with the act. Architecture reflects thought — but for us it's also the other way around. Architecture provides a particular way of seeing and speaking about things. What is important to me is that this language remains open and conceptual in nature — that it does not replace investigation and that it is able to assimilate the specific aspects of a given project. To paraphrase a thought from Nelson Goodman's *Mind and Other Matters:* architecture has to function as an institution for the prevention of blindness — allowing us to look inquisitively and to see, sharpening perception, raising visual intelligence, widening perspectives, bringing out new connections and contrasts; organizing and reorganizing experience and thus making and remaking our world.

Jean Nouvel

PROJECTS, COMPETITIONS, BUILDINGS
1980 — 1990

Good evening, I am pleased to be here in Vienna.

I should like briefly to explain to you the way my office works, and then show you some slides. I will comment in a fairly general way on relatively old projects, that is, projects which were realized about ten years ago, and then I will discuss three or four buildings of recent date in more detail.

To get a bit of background, let us take a look at architecture in France. Fifteen or twenty years ago there were two main streams, and they are still evident and alive today. First, the successor to the Modern Movement under Le Corbusier, which is to be seen mainly in the big suburban housing-estates, and secondly the historicizing, traditional direction, which soon proclaimed itself the "renewer of the European city".

As a young architect I did not feel drawn to either of these two tendencies. Consequently I had to create my own field, and this was not entirely an easy task, for I had to explain my ideas somehow. I discussed them with some friends, but the Modernists had forgotten what the Modern Movement meant: they no longer knew what a free plan, a pilotis, a window band were. So what remained? What remained were the typical parallelepipeds with a few small square windows, tiny, hyper-traditional apartments, built over and over again, all over France, all of a type. So much for the Modernists ....

And as for the others, it was a nightmare; a nightmare that became established and flourished, because French politicians wanted to avoid taking any risks with architecture. As they did not like Modernism they wanted buildings that would not catch the eye, and it was during this period that the "pseudo-Parisian" blocks were built, little white blocks with little arcades.

All this caused a certain reaction in me and some of my friends, which took form in the Mouvement Mars 1976 (March 1976 Movement). We made a stand against the way cities were being built and demanded specific approaches in urban projects. Then came the anti-competition

1. *La Tour sans Fins, Triangle de la Folie, La Défense, Paris, 1989*

for the Les Halles quarter in Paris in 1979, which tried to oppose the Chirac plan, that indescribable architectural catastrophe that has regrettably become reality: pseudo-Parisian blocks surrounding a "melting-pot"; it's quite flabbergasting. These statements of position gave me the image of a rebel, an image I still have today.

In this connection, and to explain my attitude better, I must also briefly mention the École des Beaux-Arts, an institute of "deformation," which left its mark on me, particularly in the matter of designs and plans. I'll give you an example. When they had to work out a project within twelve or eighteen hours under examination conditions, many students appeared with ready-drawn plans, which they simply copied. I always mistrusted these fine but meaningless plans, and I was the first student at the École des Beaux-Arts before 1968 to hand in a typewritten project, size 21 x 29.7 cm, which did not contain a single drawing. This was seen as a provocation, as if someone had dropped a stink-bomb, and my work did not get the marks it deserved.

The last part of this historical survey brings me to the year 1968, when the sociological and social aspects came to the fore. It was the time of "participative" architecture, when architects were concerned with the people who would live in the buildings, the private and the public weal. I was a part of all of this, and gained much valuable experience. One of the most important projects was the Ville Nouvelle in Cergy-Pontoise, where we went into the market-place and the factory canteens to talk to the families for whom we were supposed to build. I like to think back to that time; I benefited greatly from it, particularly, I would say, in that I developed certain attitudes — not least regarding the consultation process, which can be demagogic if it is not conducted under the right conditions.

Why am I telling you all this? To explain certain attitudes, which were initially, to be sure, a reaction to circumstances and real constraints. But we have tried to make that reaction positive, for ultimately it is not enough to be against something, one also has to be for something. The key element in my work is a reaction to all these modernist or historicizing proposals. My first reaction is directed against international architecture, it has to do with identity, by which I mean that every question requires an individual answer. So each time I try to identify all the reasons that induce me to build in a certain place, at a certain time, with certain people, in a certain way and no other.

This gave rise to a number of very different projects, which soon caused my opponents to label me an eclecticist . . . . It was, admittedly, a pretty dangerous attitude, for it meant rejecting the concept of style that is usually accorded the artist and the architect who makes a particular language his own and repeats it, always using the same materials and the same vocabulary of forms. In short, the idea of contextuality led me to very different projects.

I am interested in a variety of contextual factors. Firstly, as you can probably guess, there is the historical context. I love history, and because I do, I reject ersatz history of any kind. A Neogothic church will never have the perfection of a Gothic cathedral! So this context, this awareness of the here and now, of what one can realize within the frame of the present cultural and intellectual climate, is the starting-point of my work.

The second very important area is the human context. That affects both the way a project is worked out in the office and our relation to the other partners, particularly the client, and then those people on the sidelines, those who have to approve the project .... For one must not forget that architecture today is the only area of culture that is officially censored. I assume that things are no different in Austria. It is sufficient for a project not to please an inspector and it will be rejected. Inspectors, officials, entrepreneurs are some of the people we come up against, and I believe that the shape a building takes is also influenced by such people.

Naturally there is also the geographical and economic context. I am not exactly a "neoregionalist," but I do believe that certain factors connected with local know-how and techniques, or related to the cultural attitude of certain cities, or the use of materials, the climate, etc., should be taken into account. I devote particular attention to these aspects.

Then there is the cultural context, which I believe is particularly important "theoretically." One must remember that architecture is not an autonomous discipline. Saying that puts me in opposition to a lot of people in France, for the most part professors — M. Huet and M. Ciriani are probably well-known internationally. I do not believe that it is sufficient to study the history of architecture. That does not mean that one should not study it, but the key to contemporary architecture does not lie in the legacy of Ledoux or Alberti. Architecture is directly related to living culture. Creating architecture means incorporating in what is built the values of a civilization, and to do that one needs to understand that civilization, live with it. Architecture is thus in constant interplay with the culture we live in, with the fine arts, with technical, scientific and medical research, and quite generally with all the areas of the production of images. For, whether we like it or not, architecture is primarily image. One becomes aware of it through the eye; the architect is inevitably influenced by new forms that emerge, by new aesthetic approaches, even if he rejects them .... He absorbs them unconsciously, the image fixes itself in his consciousness whether he wants it to or not, and in his memory, even if it is later reworked. I believe we should not forget that.

For me, modernity is not a historical concept, derived from the Modern Movement, it is something that is alive. Modernity, the criteria of Modernity are continuously developing. I do not believe that what was modern forty or fifty years ago is automatically modern today, and this has direct consequences in architecture. Take structure, for example: it used to be modern to emphasize the way a building was built. Parameters like structural legibility and spatial definition in the geometrical sense are two criteria that are becoming less important in the modernity of today. To enter a building whose immediate message is "Look how I am made, look at my fine frame, my fine piping," is to receive a very weak message.

On space, one can say that this century has seen a fantastic process of exploration. It was once enough to appropriate a formal field to be regarded as a great artist. To be a great architect, it was once perhaps enough to have a formal language that defined a certain geometric type of space. Today, when almost everything has already been proposed or realized, what is the point of constructing a pyramidal shape based on curves, on fractured spaces? One has the impression that architecture is no longer determined by the geometrical quality of the space, that a shift has taken place. More importance is now attached to material, light, interface, that is, what one chooses to show or to hide. I am very interested in these questions.

I like to compare architecture with the cinema. The positions of the architect and the film director are very similar in many respects. They are both concerned with a project that is to be made reality, for a film is a reality, an economic reality that involves huge sums of money. Both the architect and the director are confronted with the same reality, censorship, external constraints, and they have to find a consensus. These parallels — and there are others — should induce us to re-examine our method of working. The credits to a film name a list of people who have helped to make it. If credits were given in the same way for architecture, they would be just as lengthy. Generally I try to list the people with whom I have worked. I start work by engaging the consultants needed for the project, for projects are becoming ever more complex — grand opera house, a major airport, a hospital. Clearly we have to work more and more analytically. So I begin to form special teams of architects with particular roles for each project, as with a film, which has a sound engineer, a scriptwriter, a composer, a cameraman und so on. Naturally I take the role of director, of "realizer," but my method of working is based on "brainstorming," on the spoken word. The drawings are only made later, when we know exactly what we want to do. This produces projects that have often been described as too concept-bound, as they are ultimately based more on an idea than on a tangible reality. We only come to terms with this reality later; in the first encounter with a project there are no formal constraints. The form naturally interests me, but only after the bases have been laid.

One last point. None of my projects stretches the limits of my imagination. An architect works with reality. I like to go as far as possible each time with regard to what is feasible. This is a tightrope-walk, a game with the people with whom one happens to be dealing. If one goes too far, one falls. But each of my projects has the goal of being realized. I am not a paper architect. I have never done a project simply from delight in a beautiful design. My only delight is in building. And now for some illustrations.

The first of my buildings to become known internationally was built in 1978. It is a private clinic with maternity ward (fig. 3). What is interesting about this building is that it dates more or less from the era of the Centre Pompidou, which opened two years before. It is a concrete structure, but no-one can see that. Inside one sees no supporting columns, no girders, no pipes. Nothing suggests the method of construction. Everything has been put behind the walls; it is the image that predominates.

A school on the outskirts of Paris, built around 1980 (fig. 2). In France schools were then being produced on the basis of models. That is, a building-firm and an architect would design a building, and it would be adapted by another architect. So the architect was given, in effect, a kit of parts. This school is one of these standard models. I tried to free myself of the constraints of this system and so I only retained three of the many

2. Collège d'Enseignement Secondaire Anne Frank, Antony, 1979 – 80

3. Centre Médico-Chirurgical du Val Notre Dame, Bezons, 1978

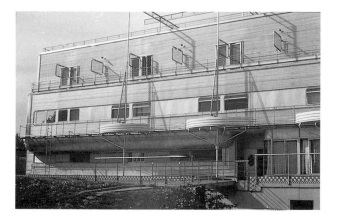

elements of the kit: a pier, a girder and a façade module. This resulted in an architecture of multiple combinations. The basic idea is not so much a system of supports as an aesthetic system. It is to be found in the lighting and on the floors, which are painted like tennis-courts. The particular feature of this project is the light: all the corridors, halls and classrooms are lit only by colored light. The children say it is "fantastic, like being in a disco."

This is an old nineteenth-century theater, which was to be converted into a cultural center incorporating other existing buildings, a social insurance office and the fire-station (fig. 4). A tower has been capped. The mayor told me the fire-station tower was too high, it should be capped. So we capped it. We cut the theatre open, as with a cleaver. Of course we had great problems obtaining permission. The public inspector from the departmental planning office said, "Over my dead body!" But the project went through, and the inspector is still alive.

A leisure center for children in Antony, a Paris suburb. This is where the children go when they have no school. I approached the project as if I were writing a children's book. The features are exaggerated as in a cartoon. We echoed motifs from Bachelard: the cellar, the store, the common-room, the motif of the tree which becomes a pillar and so on. We were very didactic in our approach and tried to stay on the children's level.

A sports hall in Ville Nouvelle, a Paris suburb, was to be the starting-point for a rondel. But that's as far as it got; I nicknamed the building "the absurd fragment."

4. Converted theatre, Belfort, 1983

This is a borderline case. The buildings were to stand on a historic site, and we were instructed to use pitched roofs and the colors blue and white. So we worked in duplicates, that is, every house was, so to speak, doubled up and given a "twin brother" (fig. 5). The signs are all inverted, the lintels are glazed, the stairs lead nowhere, blue becomes white, and so on.

Here we had to convert old farm and industrial buildings in Nîmes into a school. The work was directed by the Municipal Technical Department. I asked for an Yves Klein blue, and they used navy blue. I was so annoyed, I had wanted to develop all Klein's themes. The classrooms are blackened, in other rooms we used gold leaf, and Klein blue is back on the outside. Some of the gold foil has been gone over with the blowlamp. Each room is treated differently, but with circumspection, so it is not quite an Yves Klein room. The teachers were afraid it was the sort of building that just asked to be vandalized and smeared with graffiti, but their fears were unfounded.

Presidential competition: the Finance Ministry in Paris, a huge construction in aluminium and glass. We did not win the competition. I believe that I hold a very interesting record in France: I have lost the greatest number of competitions in the last few years.

In the presidential projects I usually obtained a distinction or second prize. This competition was won by Paul Chemetoff, and his project has now been built.

This was another competition in which I only came second — the "keystone" of the La Défense quarter. I am sure you know the winning project, which has now been built — the white cube, "la Grande Arche." My project would have, so to speak, divided the sky into windows; it was a play on perspective. The building would have been set against the horizon and the sun would have gone down behind it. I aimed to dissolve the facades, push them back within the structure (fig. 6).

7. *Centre d'Art Contemporain and Médiatheque, Nîmes, 1984*

8. *Opera house, Tokyo, Japan (with Philippe Starck), 1987*

This is a project that I both won and lost. It was to have been built, but the World Fair in Paris for the bicentenary of the French Revolution was cancelled. In this project platforms were to be constructed over the Seine between the two parts of the exhibition, east and west; this would have prevented a concentration of visitors in one site.

The project for La Grande Halle in the Parc de la Villette. To do away with the prejudice that technology and nature are irreconcilable, we maintained that a mountain is much more beautiful if a motorway crosses it and a plain is much more attractive if it is traversed by power-lines. La Villette was surrounded by fields. The program called for a thousand trees. We grouped all the trees in one place, and so solved the tree problem. We kept all the trains, railroad tracks, trucks, technical paraphernalia, barges, cranes, etc., and used them as part of the architecture, to contrast with the cornfields, trees and plantings.

The concert-hall in Bagnolet, which was built over a motorway junction. We evolved a science-fiction scenario for this. In the year 2001 a monolith, a black box, falls to the earth. It is examined by a flying laboratory which establishes that it is harmless and that communication is only possible through music. Everyone is then invited to make music here and to listen. The laboratory is a play on connotations. One hundred and fifty connotations are worked into the project, starting with trumpets, going through the carriers of a Harley-Davidson motorcycle and engine casings to theatre spotlights, theatre reflectors, etc. One hundred and fifty images are concentrated in one building.

The Médiatheque in Nîmes, opposite the well-known Roman temple, the Maison Carrée. This project also only got second prize; Norman

Foster won the international competition. Our project was to be on the level of the Roman temple, that is, below the present level, with a public place in transparent glass (fig. 7). The museum was to be below ground, and we wanted to use water as a reference to the birth of the city of Nîmes. The water was to flow over the site, under the road, under the bridge, and flow down into the museum.

Tokyo Opera House (fig. 8). A competition we lost, but lost with honor. I proposed a monolith 150 meters in length and 80 meters high, in black granite. The various rooms were given names like "Realm of the Soul," "Realm of Shades," etc. The halls decorated with gold leaf would glitter in the darkness. This tense form emanates a mystery, something that presses out from the inside. It is also a play of interface. When one enters the huge space, 110 meters in height, windows 35 meters high open on each side, making a kind of hole in the black building and creating a Magritte effect.

Another competition I lost was a "21st-century" maternity clinic for test-tube babies on a hill overlooking Paris. The clinic has a panoramic form, marking it off from the terrible hospitals of the seventies. The building looks like an instrument that has just been plugged in, a radar-station, a "ready-made" that has landed here and is observing Paris.

This is a project that did win the competition, but it was canceled six months ago. It is a large hotel with a balneotherapy center in Vichy, and it was to have been built for the Perrier company (fig. 9). The building was to link two parks, bridging the boulevards with a golden vault on which the glass bricks look like drops of water. It was to be built or clad entirely with glass bricks, even the floor.

Now a crazy project by four crazy people: a German, Otto Steindl, who is perhaps the least crazy; an Italian, who is pretty mad and is called Fuksas; an Englishman called Alsop, who is completely nuts; and a Frenchman of whom I would prefer not to speak. Alsop, the Englishman, is designing the bottom part, which looks like a fish and will accommodate shops. Fuksas is doing the lower third of the tower, in which the offices are located. Steindl is concerned with the central part, where the apartments are. I am designing a hotel on the top. The project is currently being appraised, and although the starting-point was rather venturesome we have not given up hope that it may yet be realized.

This is the project for Kansai airport, a competition that was won by Renzo Piano. Let me tell you a little anecdote: I wanted to build a kind of aircraft-carrier, that is, an artificial island of simple shape. Above all, I did not want any trees at all. Renzo Piano said artificiality yes, but with nature. And he has 2,500 trees!

The next project was designed for the city of Perpignan. It was to be a civic center with offices, apartments, three hotels, an opera-house, and a flower market. This was all promised before the elections. The project helped the party to win the election and now they can take their time in realizing it. The facades of the houses consist of large shutters, and the apartments can be fully opened. The square itself has a shape derived from the Piazza Navona, it is 250 meters long and 50 meters wide.

The Tower of Infinity, the endless tower, is the most important project we are currently working on. It is a tower 420 meters high, and is to be built beside the Grande Arche in La Défense in Paris (fig. 1). The particular features of this tower are the gradations of color and the fact that it has no base and grows out of a crater 35 meters deep. At the lower end the tower consists of matt gray granite, and as it goes up the granite becomes ever softer and shinier, then changes to a dark gray, charcoal gray, light gray, and then gives way to other materials like aluminum. The gray gets lighter until the tower ends in a cylinder that is like an empty tube without a floor. The whole project develops as the materials change, with the extremities not visible. This gives a sense of infinity. The tower is by its nature a metaphysical object, for the question of limits is a metaphysical question that concerns us all.

Now we come to a project in London. It is King's Cross station, on the big square by Norman Foster. This project is currently blocked because of Prince Charles's misgivings, and we do not believe that it will be realized in the near future. It is a large greenhouse, for all the beams are under a glass roof, which is closed on one side. The water of the canal enters the construction from below, creating a play with the light that enters between the two reflecting walls.

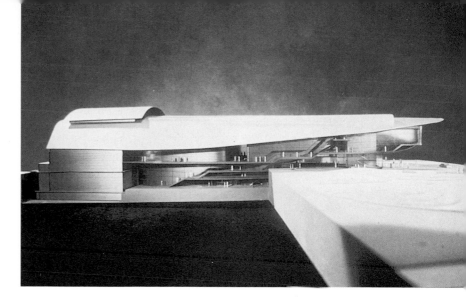

10. Palais des Congrès, Tours, 1989

This is the project in Rotterdam on which we are working now. A harbor site, about thirty hectares in size, on which the municipal heating works once stood. Actually it is a city within a city. We tried to create a certain distance by not building over the entire slope. As one approaches one sees the silhouette of a city rising in the middle of a city.

The project for the Grande Bibliothèque, a presidential competition. I did not win it, the winner was Dominique Perrault. However, the project was given a special mention by the jury. The design is based on an inhabited bridge and the notion of the tree. My proposal was for a large library to develop over about two hundred years, with buildings being grafted onto branches, which are wide boulevards covered with great gilt ceilings, which would display work by the greatest artists of our time.

A project for the jewelers Cartier near Fribourg in Switzerland, beside a motorway. The project bears Cartier's trademark, which is shown as both a positive and a negative image, as in a mirror.

This is a second-prize project, that is, another competition I did not win. It was a French-Japanese competition for a monument to be given to Japan by France, as we once gave the Americans the Statue of Liberty. I proposed a kind of magma video in a hole, a construction like a volcano, on which a mirror is placed that reflects the video picture. The mirror turns with the sun, so that the picture is always entirely in the shade. The picture is like a flame, an image in the sky over the Bay of Osaka. It was to be a pantheon in which the most important images of our century were perpetuated: Armstrong on the moon, the DNS molecule and what have you ....

Another competition I did win. This is the Congress Center at Tours, which consists of three halls with capacities of 2,000, 800 and 400 seats.

11. *Institut du Monde Arabe, Paris, 1987. Stairs*

12. *Institut du Monde Arabe, Paris, 1987*

13. *Institut du Monde Arabe, Paris, 1987. Patio*

They open into each other. The complex also includes an office building. It forms the gateway to the city when you come from the station (fig. 10).

Now to some aspects of the Institut du Monde Arabe in Paris (figs. 11, 12). The north building, which is mainly a museum and follows the bend in the Seine, and the south building, in which a public library is located, are separated by a cleft. The word "institute" is not a very fortunate choice, because this is actually a cultural center like the Centre Pompidou. It has the same kind of program, but is only one third the size. The building houses temporary exhibitions, a museum, a library and a lecture-theater. In our concept we aimed to embody the characteristics of great Arab architecture: light and geometry. All these Arab forms, the star, the polygon, the square, can be reduced by rotation. The blinds are computerized, the computer receives commands through a photocell linked to a thermometer: the blinds open and close, depending on whether it is raining or sunny. The most difficult task was to explain to the client that this construction was not a simple curtain blind but a light-control mechanism, which is naturally much more expensive. An electrified Venetian blind would of course have been much simpler, much more efficient and much cheaper — but it would have been no fun at all. For the first time technology has been harnessed and money spent purely for pleasure. We wanted to give pleasure to the people who were to live in this building, we wanted proper light control, with geometrical shadows. And we succeeded this time in selling sensation instead of function.

The inside court: In the center of the building is a white marble cube, consisting of thousands of small, fine marble wafers. The light shines through these as through alabaster. There was to be a mercury fountain in the center, but it has not yet been realized; a mirror has taken its place (fig. 13).

The entrance-hall: This is one of the special effects. It is thirty meters high and leads into a hall two meters high. The derivation from the columned halls in mosques is very evident.

Now to a social housing complex in St. Ouen, near Paris. For fifteen years I didn't have the chance to build social housing. My philosophy on social housing can be reduced to one sentence: a beautiful room is a big room, it is an aesthetic criterion, and a beautiful apartment is a large apartment. Starting from this idea I aimed to construct larger units for the same price, and for that reason I kept everything very simple. The façades are very economical and industrially fabricated. The apartments have direct access and the inside is large and white.

More social housing in Nîmes, above the city. Two large ships protected from the sun by umbrellas (fig. 14). There are also two terraces, one open to the public, the other private. One sees the sky through the umbrellas. This transparency is also to be found on the balconies. The public terraces and the stairs are in the sun. The small red lights on the terraces bathe everything in red light in the evening. The façades can be fully opened if the weather is fine, and the balcony and living-room becomes one room. One can actually put furniture out without it seeming ridiculous (fig. 15). Everything is generously proportioned. For the raw concrete I engaged one of my friends, who is an artist, to paint it. The client said, stop, we will never be able to let these. So we only painted about forty percent of the apartments, but half of the other tenants, who did not have any painting, wanted some. So we triumphed.

14. Social housing, Nemausus 1 – 114, Nîmes, 1987.

15. Social housing, Nîmes, 1987. Balcony and living room

And that is a very special thing in Nîmes, because the term "triumph" is used in bullfighting.

This is a cultural center in Ville Nouvelle, near Paris. These "new towns" are like collections of models. Each architect who comes puts up a different kind of building. So I looked at the surrounding buildings and designed mine accordingly. The wealth of forms is a reflection of the surroundings. I tried to create contrasts between the black theater auditoriums and the publicly accessible areas or the library, which are transparent. In the evening everything is bathed in blue light.

In 1989 we built a luxury hotel near an old church above Bordeaux. At the foot of the hill one can see the river Garonne. It is a small village, and so I built small houses. The houses are rust-colored, and have small electric shutters (fig. 16). This is the bar. It is all very well finished, as usual. The photographs in the background show the site before the building-work.

One of the rooms. It is all white (fig. 17). The beds are very high, as is usual in the country, 110 cm. Lying in bed one has a view over the whole city. The armchairs we designed are very comfortable. What I particularly like here is the correspondence between the bathtub and the bed.

16. Hotel Restaurant Saint-James, Bordeaux, 1989

17. Hotel Restaurant Saint-James, Bordeaux, 1989. Hotel room

And now a documentation center in Nancy. This is our latest project. The center is a place where knowledge is transformed and collected. Knowledge is sent here from all over the world, collected, collated, translated and passed on to researchers. I won the competition for this project three or four years ago. My competitors wanted to build office buildings, while I created a factory. The building is really like a factory, a factory in which the raw material knowledge is processed (figs. 18, 19).

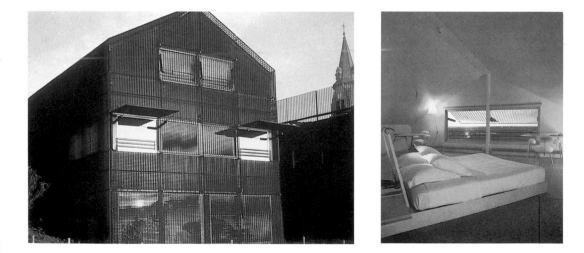

18. *Centre de Documentation du CNRS, Nancy, 1989*

19. *Centre de Documentation du CNRS, Nancy, 1989*

The center is a building for the end of this century; it is all based on a very exact organization plan, through which the functions are directly accessible. I call this beauty through efficiency. The building in which the archive is located is split throughout its entire height. The EDP building is made entirely of chrome-plated steel.

This is the interior of the EDP building. Upstairs is a restaurant and above that the administrative area. All we need now is the greenery.

Michael Sorkin

NINETEEN MILLENNIAL MANTRAS

During his years in office, Ronald Reagan came to be nicknamed the "Teflon President" after the plastic coating used on pots and pans to prevent food from sticking to them during cooking. Reagan acquired this sobriquet because no matter how deceitful his behavior, no matter how many transparent lies he uttered, no accusation seemed to stick to him; however often they were reported in the press, proofs of his mendacity were never persuasive to his adoring public.

Over time, Reagan became a kind of sublime epistemological conundrum, a riddling sphinx. It was impossible to see his ubiquitous face without worrying about the very origins and reliability of knowledge itself. From his dyed hair, to his genial hypocrisy to his bald-faced lies, every aspect of Reagan seemed to beg the question of the nature of truth. By the time of the Iran-Contra scandal near the end of his second term, the inquiry had come to be embodied in a pithy incantation repeated over and over by virtually all who cared: "What did the President know? And when did he know it?"

This proved to be the crucial formulation of Reaganism. By introducing the aspect of temporality — "When did he know it?" — the media arrived at a summary of the Reagan riddle that took into account both the fact of his monumental dishonesty and the incredibly abiding love that the American people persisted in harboring for him, a love that simply refused to see his lies as lies. The new construction solved the puzzle by moving the site of the question from the terrain of ethics to the territory of memory. Reagan's actions could thereby be dismissed as merely the difficulties of senility, the innocent failings of an old man, a medical problem. Tacitly acknowledging this, Reagan developed a mirror refrain of his own, repeated at every press conference, deposition, and photo op: "I can't recall."*

The great irony in all of this is that Reagan was the first true postmodernist politician: his politics were symbolized precisely by his own longevity. Reagan came to power as the great apostle of memory, prom-

---

1. Model City, analogue relief plan, 1989

ising Americans a return to a golden age, a time to which his years allegedly gave him special access. This mock vision of Elysium infected all fields of culture, including architecture. During the Reagancy, memory emerged as the most powerful complicit value in architectural discourse. From historicist theories of the city to the revolting classical reminiscences of endless Neo-Con building projects to the Disneyfication of most of material culture, the stench of the so-called "past" everywhere crowded out the perfume of invention and experiment.

If architecture has a crisis — and I believe that it has — it is a crisis of authenticity, a crisis about locating value in an age of simulation, the same crisis that produced Reagan, the simulated President. Under this phony regime, everything is thrown into undecidability. The commercial asks, "Is it real or is it Memorex?" as the recording of Ella Fitzgerald shatters the glass. Or, consider the following. One of my favorite artifacts of the Reagan era is an American television program called "Puttin' On the Hits." The show is, in effect, a lip-syncing competition. Participants dress up as some venerated popstar and proceed to simulate one of Madonna's or — more to the point — Milli Vanilli's greatest hits. In format, "Putting' On the Hits" simulates the kind of simulations one sees on shows like "American Bandstand" or "Soul Train," shows on which actual popstars lip-sync to their own recorded performances, imitating themselves performing. Of course the situation is really even more complicated because the "authentic" performance at the source of this great chain of simulations has no actual autonomous existence, being something that was elaborately constructed from various tracks laid down in the sound studio.

At the end of these simulated simulated simulated performances, a panel of judges — marshaling an incredible array of completely spurious expertise — numerically rates the contestants in categories like "originality." Here we are getting close to the heart of the matter. The problem with "Putting' On the Hits" as a cultural model isn't the lip-sync: the real problem is with these judges, with the way in which they naturalize the fakery in terms of familiar routines of authority, some standard beyond whim or taste meant to assure us that the ersatz is just like the "real" thing. The field of consumption is dominated by such assurances, for instance the claim that the petrochemical slime purveyed at McDonald's really is nutritious, "natural" — or should I say "strong" — food.

Clearly, though, if we're going to avoid having this rammed down our throats, we need some standards for judging, however personal. This is the challenge of a culture dominated by television, the medium that begs the most fundamental questions for architecture. My favorite metaphor for contemporaneity is that good old Surrealist entertainment, the Exquisite Corpse. You know the one: Breton described it as "a game of folded paper played by several people who compose a sentence or drawing without anyone seeing the preceding collaboration or collaborations." The now classic example, which gave the game its name, was the first sentence obtained this way: "The exquisite corpse will drink new wine." The Surrealists held this game in high esteem. "Finally," wrote Breton, "we had at our command an infallible way of holding the critical intellect in abeyance, and of fully liberating the mind's metaphorical activity."

The Exquisite Corpse is a primitive juxtaposition-machine, a means of literary or artistic gene-splicing. It aims to break down conventional structures of meaning by declaring that anything goes with anything. Television is a sophisticated juxtaposition-machine. Contemplate for a moment the actual experience of television. Whether it's produced by the remote control zap or the flânerie of the daily schedule, the cut is television's main event, producing an unbelievable miasma of ever more minuscule bits, fragment after fragment after fragment. Like the playing of the Exquisite Corpse, every watching of television yields an astonishing, totally original artifact, a fresh freak. That characteristic jump from the rotting bodies in Basra to the douche commercial ought to be ludicrous but it's not. And this juxtaposition reveals the power of modern culture, the power to make true and false obsolete. Breton would be amazed.

For consumerism — which seeks simply to maximize the available number of things — this system for eroding the inflexibilities of meaning is amazingly economical. After all, if any justaposition makes sense, no combination is lost. It's just like those infinite monkeys sitting at their typewriters, pecking away until one of them finally produces *Hamlet*. The only problem with that system is the implied waste of paper before the Bard is successfully aped. Television resolves this difficulty with bold economy. Since there can be no illegible artifacts, every chimp's a Shakespeare. By extension, any accident can be President . . . or architecture. Indeed, the freak is the characteristic reconciliation of simulation and authority.

Don't get me wrong, I love the abundance and there's nothing wrong with being a freak. What's missing here — what the TV system prefers you not to have — is a useful, truly meaningful system for distinguishing, for working through it all. The Surrealists, of course, had Surrealism: they wanted their images to be screwy and presumably examined the products of their juxtaposition-machine for traces of familiarity. But what are we to do? Take a look at this Hollywood image,

the very latest in the constructed subject! Michael Jackson and E.T. are — along with Ronald Reagan, Mickey Mouse, and Chairman Mao — easily the most mediated images of the age. Michael and E.T. are linked not simply as embodiments of the cuddly Other but due precisely to the degree of their mediation: they're neighbors in the same conceptual space. Fabulous furry freak brothers, they belong together precisely because anything belongs together on their planet. This universal coincidence is a recipe for inertia, for sitting there and changing the channel again and again and again and again.

Architecture must somehow account for this unruly realm or die. The anything-goes space of simulation has the power to overwhelm architecture in two fundamental ways. First, by the creation of a so-called "virtual reality" that is as persuasive and mesmerizing in its sensory effects as anything we're able to produce at the drawing-board. We must eventually decide whether this electronic, hallucinogenic space is to be the new space of architecture — but more about this later. More immediately serious is the promiscuous pluralism of the consumer juxta-position-machine, the fearsome repression of absolute tolerance which makes ludicrous virtually any decision that we make, short of total surrender. Classicism today, Deconstructivism tomorrow — who gives a fuck, it's only images.

What resources do we architects have against this? Obviously a critical stance is crucial. To paraphrase Lenin, patience and irony are the chief virtues of a true architect. But beyond critique, I think it's crucial for each of us to ask the kiddie's first question: where do buildings come from? Every architect, in his or her formation, must invent architecture afresh: we all need our primal scenes. Beyond the requirements of good citizenship and respect for the planet, this necessitates the organization of some system of preferences, some serious self-emboldening as to the sources of the answer. Nowadays, there's a struggle over the organization of these preferences into doctrines, an impulse to arrogate the authority of other systems to give an absolute account for taste. Like the man on TV testifying about the weight-loss formula that allowed him to lose two hundred pounds, architects everywhere give endless accounts of their procedures . . . "I drew a line from Freud's house to the Michaelerplatz, I read Calvino, I rotated the grid the same number of degrees as it was Celsius on the afternoon that I met you, I spat on the drawing, I traced the outline of last night's schnitzel," etc., etc.

This kind of daffy, postfunctionalist methodology (form follows . . . . anything!) is probably as good a place to begin as there is. I like the talk just fine — it's the piety that's disturbing. For me, sources give no special authority to forms, however much they may veneer a layer of curiosity or provide fodder for graduate students and psychoanalysts. Still, where else can you begin? What, finally, is there really to talk about other than intentions and whims? In this spirit I'd like to present a series of theses, my own intentions and whims. But "theses" is too overbearing a word. Rather, let me offer some mantras, some chants to use in confronting the ever looming crisis of beginnings. These mantras lead nowhere in particular: I don't think this is really the moment for prescription, certainly not at the formal level. We scarcely need to assert the universal necessity of pilotis and a free ground-plane, the superiority of regionalism, the importance for architecture of expressing in its every beam and joist the destabilized character of modern social relations. My mantras are simply sites, spots where architecture seems especially fluid to me, the places where I'm thinking about architecture, the advice I give myself. As someone who sees himself in a condition of just starting, I choose also to give them a swelling millennial tone, in the expectation that a decade will carry me somewhere. These mantras are both hopeful and cautionary.

1. If Words Fail, Grunt

To begin the game, you've got to put the signifier into play. Fold paper, close your eyes, stab the dictionary, pick your nose and examine the product carefully, watch TV day and night, look up your ass with a mirror. Although we all crawl before we fly, architecture is no universal language, not for long at any rate. It's true, though, that useful beginnings will tend to be on all fours, the most modest statical condition. Later we learn to boogie.

2. Cyberspace Isn't (Or Is It?)

As I suggested earlier, if architecture as we know it is threatened by millennial technical change, it's because the gremlins of DNA and silicon and the wizards of aerospace and entertainment — the military-industrial-biological-themepark complex — are increasingly able to provide experiences of simulated spatiality that are ever more indistinguishable from the "real thing." Walter Wriston — ex-CEO of Citibank — recently remarked on television: "The 800 telephone-number and the piece of plastic have made time and space obsolete." Or, as Don De Lillo has a character say in his novel *White Noise:* "For most people there are only two places in the world, where they live and their TV set. If something happens on TV, they have the right to find it fascinating, whatever it is." Who needs Ronchamp when you have the Cosby Show. I don't mean to sound the Luddite, but I do believe that the retention of literal physicality will be one of the great crises of architecture in the coming century. On the other hand, if virtual reality turns out to be better, more useful, more under our control, more profoundly connected to the lebenswelt, who needs architecture!

3. No More Second-Hand Space

Speaking of the simulacrum, isn't architecture getting a tad onanistic? There's a narcissism abroad, a tightening gyre of self-simulation. Our feeble, coopted avant-garde — caught up completely in the routines of the gallery system — takes itself much too seriously, obsessed with pedigree, giving endless whimpering accounts — fawning, awful declarations of sensitivity — stupidly offering its tattooed seriousness as vaccine against further Nagasakis and Treblinkas. Let's stop this. The hermeneutics of nothingness can only yield the architecture of despair.

It's another millennial symptom, a crisis of authority striking a class of production nervous about its own irrelevance. Recent Frankenstein attempts to graft the purloined authority of theory and history onto the comatose body of unexamined architecture have — to date — not even managed to produce any particularly worthwhile freaks, just Stalinoid baubles foaming about how true they are. Slathered with decon mascara or ratsy rouge, the content doesn't change, despite the claim. The result:

an architecture obsessed with buggering flies and telling the rest of us not to have good sex. Why this nervousness in front of teacher when it would be better just to have fun? Here's a good formula for judging architectural results: that's the way — uh-huh uh-huh — that's the way I like it.

4. No More Second-Hand Superego

I don't exactly know why your unconscious should become my folklore. Why should anyone be bothered by the return of someone else's re-pressed? Once we're adults, we can try to be clear about the engines that regulate us, we can fight to make a choice. If you'd rather have Einstein than the Brothers Grimm at bedtime, so be it! If you prefer Chaka Khan to Jacques Lacan, let's disco! Some caution, however, seems prudent. There's somebody under that Mickey Mouse costume and it isn't clear that he's friendly. Whenever we dance, I think I feel his grip on my wallet. Go to hell, Mickey! An architect needs sharp teeth, ready to bite the invisible hand.

5. Free Mimesis

A few sights that interest me: the strange conjoined expressionistic planes of the Stealth fighter; the weird attenuated snout, darting long tongue, and push-me, pull-you body of the anteater; the billowing of clouds; the way navigation devices are grafted to the sides of airplanes like goiters; crepuscular blue skies; almost any construction site; the little knobs on brioche; extremely long flights of stairs; dinosaurs, especially stegosaurus; the heliotropic bending of trees in the city; long hairs that sprout from little bumps on the cheeks of dogs. Like all art, architecture is happiest when it loves the world. Like all art, function follows form.

6. You Can't Dance to a Bad Beat

Naturally though, function shouldn't follow form anywhere. Taste is not an absolute substitute for thinking, never mind how elaborately it's rationalized. If anyplace, Vienna is a reminder that the waltz is only one beat away from the march. Is it possible to love both? Only with some changes: all fantasies of cooporation are not the same, there's good sex and bad. My own deepest pornographic fascination — as you may have gathered — is with aircraft, with needle-nosed fighters, swing-winged bombers, and hulking, bulbous transports. Such aesthetic fancies are mighty troubled. After all, these are implements with no good uses, murder-weapons. While generalissimos at the Pentagon may stare with untroubled satisfaction at velvet paintings of sunsets streaked with B-52 contrails, slavering with the same unalloyed scopophilia as the teen boy crouched over the centerfold of Miss October, the rest of us — neither futurists nor fascists — encounter greater difficulty with these images. The answer's the *détournement*, dancing to the march, turning the sergeant-major into Sergeant Pepper, wearing their clothes on our bodies. Functionalism begins with fun.

7. Forget Gravity

Ah, yes. One of the glories of the age is that — for the first time — architecture is about to be loosed from its most primary and historic constraint: gravity. The vast project of extraterrestrial construction, already begun, proceeds almost entirely without us. Aren't we fools to be missing out? I, for one, want to participate, to go to that place where up and down cease to constrain, where our own motion can assume any angle at all. Creating an earth-bound architecture decorated with signifiers of this possibility — hanging columns and wiggly walls — is not enough; we need to be there. Free coordinates — an architecture able to find any geometry it can imagine and striving for none — beckon off the horizon. The tyranny of the grid — that great totem of the right of all modern citizens to surrender their differences — is about to be breakable. The plan has ceased to be the generator.

8. Hack, Hack, Hack

Architecture exercises its morality by its scrupulous choice of means. The brick does not choose what it wishes to be, we tell it and we don't have to tell it the same thing twice. Of course, our choice has influences — culture, diet, drugs, psychosis, etc., the usual conspiracy against the unexpected. Technology is simply more culture, it isn't received or inevitable: science is what we make it. Every technology useful to architecture must be vigorously questioned with every single use, if only to keep up with the breathy pace of change. Our prejudice must always be for better or more fun solutions: let culture play the conservative while we swing out over the void. The weight of a billion bricks laid up through history ought not to deny the billowing strong gossamer film, the tensile metallic sinews or the solar-powered electronic thermal regulator being born today in the labs of invention. Hackers, those happy Robin Hoods of appropriated technology, whizzing down the wire-print byways of the computer web, are models for us: in control, critical, ready to crash bad systems, out for good times, independent yet happy to network for what's right, for freedom and sound choices. Let us adopt the motto of the hacker as he or she penetrates to the next circle of shrouded mystery: "Further!"

9. Do What Comes Naturally

Every day is earth-day for architecture. A planetary view demands an architecture that knows both how to assert and how to recede. Terrestrial architecture, after all, is different from what we'll make off earth. Down here, the goal must be inclusion: the fantasy of regulation is unhealthy, father of pesticides and panopticons and grids without end, amen. Architecture must be green, must open its windows to let things in and out, must collaborate in the cycles that would happen without us. I sing a song of fuzzy buildings, happy to blur the edges between themselves and the woods, bored with the old arguments about distinction. I sing a song of ecology, of buildings certain of their roots, of their rejection of that zero-sum game where any building's rise has a companion depletion someplace unseen by those who have always kept their eyes pressed tight against such thoughts. Why should we still be scarring the earth — architecture wants to be about renewal. Let it blossom. Let us soon grow our buildings from seeds.

10. If It's Broke, Fix It

What are buildings for, if not use? Architecture for architecture's sake is just masturbation, no closer to the matter than a novel or a smooth stone. However inspirational a grain of sand can be, it's only a goad, not an answer: the world's just not in there. Today, especially around the schools, there's a grim, daft reticence about architecture's utility. Beleaguered by a threatening technical supersession, architecture's true defense is not to diffuse itself into an ever-expanding field, conflating with sculpture or cinema or philosophy or gardening, surrendering the brilliant abiding fact that it really is useful, that it keeps us warm, dry, curious, hidden, wet, in, out, safe, and at risk, to vague formulations about poetry or cosmology. Don't get me wrong — the whole thing works only if form has real autonomy, if it's born free. But to suppress the million happinesses of inhabitation is suicide. Architecture is strong medicine and we're the doctor. Why take the dose if you don't feel better afterwards?

11. Less Is Less

Are you as bored with minimalism as I am, with these tired old men flogging their empty boxes as if they were the containment-vessels of profundity? There comes a time when that little square ceases to look like nothingness and begins to look like a little square, when we grow tired of staring at the naked emperor's dick, however big. What's wanted now is what engineers — our ridiculously successful sibling rivals — call elegance. There's a fine and abiding idea about minimalism here. Not the dumb, meaning-pared, Limbo minimalism of the art world — that how-low-can-you-go, paranoid-about-complexity minimalism — but the isomorphic minimalism of aerospace or machine tools. The point is to find purpose that abets form, form that abets purpose, the complexity that comes from demanding that architecture do everything that we want it to even as strange new complexities invite us to want more and more. If it's complicated let's have complication, fusion, not fission, more analogies, an endless game of egging on and I-dare-you. Let us have an architecture of raised expectations and ceaseless elaboration.

12. Back to the City

The city invents architecture. It is the engine and laboratory of human relationships, a pattern computer, a Rosetta Stone. Over the past twenty years there's been a shift in architecture's understanding of the city. Nowadays, the city is too much mere mnemonic, not enough terrain of invention and art. We love Borges but don't see the city as he does, convolute and mysterious. We merely see Borges looking at the city and we shut our eyes in imitation of the blind man's gaze. Designing cities has become little more than the pseudo-psychoanalysis of elderly forms. We arrive at the office. The corpse is on the couch. After fifty minutes we say, "I'm afraid your time is up." But the analysand is no Lazarus. He just lies there and the stink gets worse and worse.

Enough of this. It's time for architecture to reembolden itself in the face of the city, to reengage the act of imagining new cities, invented from scratch, the vast possibilities for new relationships liberated by fresh technologies of propinquity, by happier visions. We didn't live through Woodstock, May '68, Tienanminh Square, just to go back to living with our parents in the suburbs. Modern urbanism has provided the world with a vast legacy of diminished expectations. If architecture has a single duty, it is precisely to raise as many of them as we can, and keep raising them, even when Daddy and Mommy say no. The new city, invented by induction, growing just out of control, needs as many centers as there are citizens.

13. Tail Wags Dog

Raising hopes may be the whole game. One of architecture's historic poignancies — and one of its charms — has been that its reach so often exceeds its grasp. I'm a Lamarckian about this. I think that overreaching — like the giraffe straining to nibble the tender leaves at the tree-top — is the only way to grow tall. Try as it will, architecture has never been able to truly invent human relations, however brilliantly it maps or wraps them. No, the most we can really do through building is to everywhere inlay a multitude of canny little distortions, provoking insights and twists, flea-bites on the doggy politic that cause it to shift and wiggle, and scratch like a mad dog. Enough of such excitement makes a new hound. Once he's heard Chubby Checker, Fido wants to twist again. Fortunately, much of this activity will appear to be funny. Terrific, I say. Let us have lots of hilarious architecture. Let us blow away the awful burdens of seriousness in gales of laughter.

14. Embody the Body

The human subject is architecture's center. This is literally true, no metaphor. Architecture is not designed around a recollection or an image, but to serve a fact, two-legged and vertical, air-breathing and susceptible to colds, happy and afraid, full of moods. Nonhabitable architecture is a perfect oxymoron. This means that all building (and unbuilding) is finally prosthetic, about extension, about extra eyes and ears, big new noses, long sinewy legs, vast foliate lungs. If architecture provides no enhancement to experience, who needs it! Otherwise, let its tasks be taken up by other arts. The only trouble with architecture prosthetically imagined is that it does create the risk of a certain monstrosity. We don't want our architecture making us into robots, shrinking our possibilities by leeching out space and leaving us narcoleptic, walkmen in our ears and remote control TV zapper-boxes in our hands. The answer's to keep working, priming our pumps: more will always be more. But I repeat: let's not spend too much time in front of the mirror. Architecture wants to be anthropomorphic in content but not always form — wo/man is not the only measure, just the only reason.

15. Mutatis Mutandis

As culture's complexity burgeons we need a hedge against too much order. Architecture ought to be fallible and richly flawed. We should always imagine architecture and our ways of making it with a boundary of apraxia, a place where it breaks down, ceases to work, a point of failure where the system reaches a complexity beyond which it can no longer perform coordinated movements. There is such a thing as too much architecture: buildings that overreach should crash and burn, lie on their backs like crabs overturned, all flailing legs and vulnerability, anxious frustration, easy prey. Every home should have a memento of some foolish collapsed tower, some bauble from Babel.

16. Just Say No

Can we have stimulus without addiction? Can architecture be more like a sweater than a syringe? Not an ordinary sweater, of course, but an exceptional sweater, a thrilling sweater, cozy, useful, glamorous, and unexpected. A sweater beyond sweaters, from a closet full of fabulous sweaters. The best pleasures are chosen, not compulsory. Tyranny is at bay only so long as we can freely remember or not remember. There will, after all, be many days when we'll want no sweater at all.

17. Ugly Architecture

Ugly is what the fearful call the new. This being the case, let's not shrink from the occasional act of reasoned terror. The main tyranny in the world is the conspiracy to save us from every unpredictability. Genetic screening allows us to abort the fetus that hasn't the brainpower for Harvard or the reflexes for a goalie. The shopping-mall makes sure all our choices are equivalent, everywhere. Perestroika guarantees a Pepsi for everyone. Let architecture rise in the defense of unreasonable fantasy: too much Pepsi or none! Architects should be wild for sex, coupling with whom or whatever's willing, climaxing like crazy. To be a great architect is to love all your kids, especially for their differences. Let us make grotesque, Rabelaisian, crazy architecture. As Bakhtin reminds us, this is the mode of regeneration and utopia, a gay parody of the official styles of reason. I like an architecture that thumbs its nose.

18. Everyone Architect

Why do we guard our prerogatives so jealously? Why not surrender them instead? Architecture, after all, is common property. How can it be then that we are so white, so male, so nicely dressed? And why, finally, do so few people really know us at our best?

19. Architecture without End

An optimistic, millennial ending: as long as we have ink on our hands the end is not nigh.

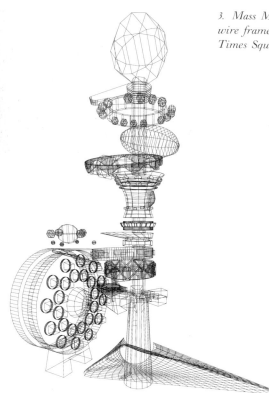

3. Mass Movement,
wire frame,
Times Square, 1990

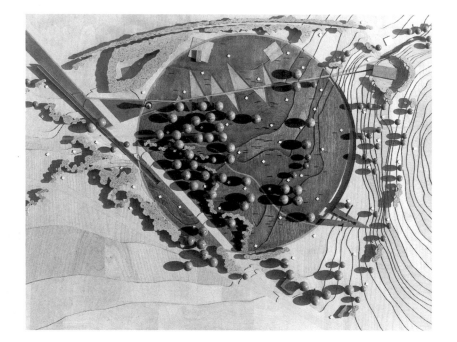

4. Parque Los
Olivos, Mexico
City, site plan
(day), 1990

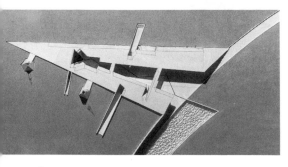

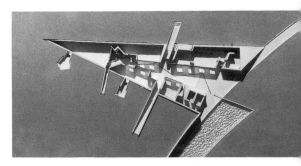

5. *Youth Center, roof plan view, (roof on), Parque Los Olivos, Mexico City, 1990*

6. *Youth Center, roof plan view, (roof off), Parque Los Olivos, Mexico City, 1990*

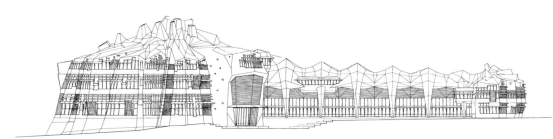

7. *Rancho Mirage City Hall, Rancho Mirage, California, elevation, 1990*

8. *Tracked Housing, New York City, 1990*

9. *Frog, Animal
Houses (2), 1991*

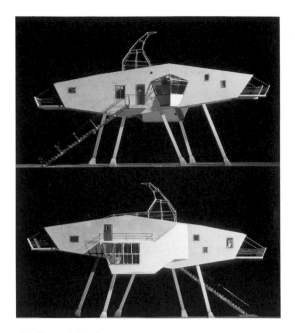

10. *Dog, Animal
Houses (1), 1990*

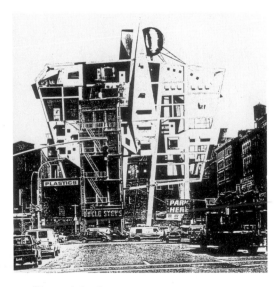

11. *Sheep, Animal
Houses (5),
Soho, New York,
1991*

12. *Aardvark,
Animal Houses (8),
photocopy 1991*

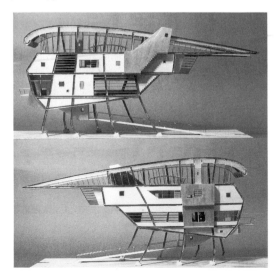

13. *Sheep, Animal Houses (5), Yosemite, 1991*

14. *Sheep, Animal Houses (5), detail, 1991*

15 *Pickle, Hanseatic Skryscraper (5), Hamburg, 1991*

Kansai Airport, Osaka — *[signature]* 88

Bernard Tschumi

EVENT ARCHITECTURE

Architecture is as much about the event that takes place in a space as about the space itself. In today's world where railway-stations become museums and churches become nightclubs, we must come to terms with the extraordinary interchangeability of form and function, the loss of traditional or canonical cause-and-effect relationships as sanctified by modernism.

Function does not follow form, form does not follow function, or fiction for that matter. However, form and function certainly interact, if only to produce a shock-effect.

If "shock" cannot be produced by the succession and juxtaposition of façades and lobbies any more, maybe it can be produced by the juxtaposition of events that take place behind these façades in these spaces.

If "the respective contamination of all categories, the constant substitutions, the confusion of genres" as described by critics of the right and the left alike (from Andreas Huyssens to Jean Baudrillard) is the new direction of our times, it may well be used to one's advantage, to the advantage of a general rejuvenation of architecture. If architecture is both concept and experience, space and use, structure and superficial image (nonhierarchically), then architecture should cease to separate these categories and should merge them into unprecedented combinations of programs and spaces. "Crossprogramming," "transprogramming," "disprogramming": these concepts stand for the displacement and mutual contamination of terms.

My own work in the seventies constantly reiterated the thesis that there was no architecture without event, without action, without activities, without functions; architecture was to be seen as the combination of spaces, events and movements, without any hierarchy or precedence among these concepts. Needless to say, the hierarchical cause-and-effect relationship between function and form is one of the great certainties of architectural thinking — it lies behind that reassuring *idée reçue* of community life that tells us that we live in houses "designed to answer

---

1. *New Kansai International Airport,*
Osaka. Photogram, 1988

to our needs" or in cities planned as machines to live in. And the cozy connotations of this *Geborgenheit* notion go against both the real "pleasure" of architecture, in its unexpected combinations of terms, and the reality of contemporary urban life, in its most stimulative, as well as unsettling, facets. Hence, in works like the *Manhattan Transcripts*, the definition of architecture could not be form, or walls, but had to be the combination of heterogenous and incompatible terms.

The incorporation of the terms "event" and "movement" was no doubt influenced by Situationist discourses and by the '68 era. "Les événements," as they were called, were events not only in action, but also in thought. Erecting a barricade (function) in a Paris street (form) is not quite equivalent to being a *flaneur* (function) in that same street (form). Dining (function) in a university hall (form) is not quite equivalent to reading or swimming in it. Here, all hierarchical relationships between form and function cease to exist.

This unlikely combination of events and spaces was charged with subversive capabilities, for it challenged both the function and the space: such confrontation parallels the Surrealists' meeting of the bicycle and the umbrella on the dissecting-table. We find it today in Tokyo, with its multiple programs scattered throughout the floors of the high-rise buildings: department-store, museum, health-club, railway-station, and putting-greens on the roof. And we will find it in the programs of the future, where airports are also simultaneously amusement-arcades, athletic-facilities, cinemas, shopping centers and so on. Regardless of whether they are the result of chance combinations or of the pressures of ever rising land prices, such noncausal relationships between form and function, or space and action, go beyond poetic confrontations of unlikely bedfellows.

2. New Kansai International Airport, Osaka. Photogram, 1988

*3. New Kansai
International
Airport, Osaka.
Photogram, 1988*

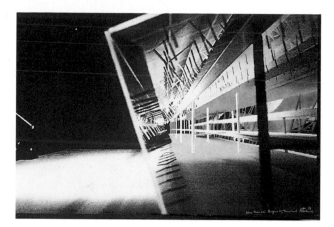

Foucault, as recalled in an excellent recent book by John Rajchman, expanded the use of the term "event" in a manner that went beyond the single action or activity. He spoke of "events of thought." I would suggest that the future of architecture today lies in the construction of such events. For Foucault, an event is not simply a logical sequence of words or actions, but rather "the moment of erosion, collapse, questioning or problematization of the very assumptions of the setting within which a drama may take place — occasioning the chance or possibility of another, different setting" (Rajchman). The event is seen here as a *turning-point*, not an origin or an end (as opposed to propositions such as "form follows function").

Just as important is the spatialization that goes with the event. To quote Foucault: "There are events in the space we construct ourselves to inhabit: heterotopia." Such a concept is, of course, quite different from the ethos of the Modern Movement, which sought to affirm certainties in a unified utopia, as opposed to our current occupation with multiple, fragmented, dislocated terrains.

After Foucault, Derrida expanded on the definition of "event," calling it "the emergence of a disparate multiplicity" in a text about the *folies* of the Parc de la Villette. I had constantly insisted, in our discussions and elsewhere, that these points called *folies* were points of activities, of programs, of events. Derrida elaborated this concept, proposing the possibility of an "architecture of the event" that would "eventalize," or open up, what in our history or tradition is understood to be fixed, essential, monumental.

Derrida had also suggested earlier that the word "event" shared roots with "invention." I would like to associate it with the notion of "shock," a shock that in order to be effective in our mediated culture, in our

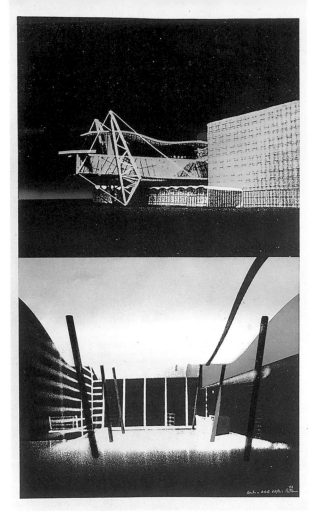

4. *American
Library, Berlin.
Photogram, 1988*

culture of *images*, must go beyond the definition of Walter Benjamin and *combine the idea of function or action with that of image.* Indeed, architecture finds itself in a unique situation: it is the only discipline that by definition combines concept and experience, image and use, image and structure. Philosophers can write, mathematicians can develop virtual spaces, but architects are the only ones who are the prisoners of that hybrid art where the image hardly ever exists without a combined activity.

It is my contention that far from being a field suffering from the incapability of questioning its structures and foundations, architecture is the field where the greatest discoveries will take place in the next century. The very heterogeneity of the definition of architecture — space, action and movement — makes it that *event*, that place of shock, or that place of the invention of ourselves. The event is the place where the rethinking and reformulation of the different elements of architec-

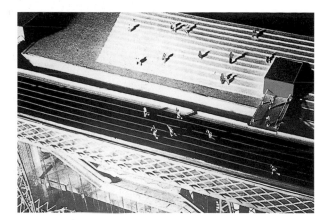

ture (many of which have resulted in, or added to, contemporary social inequities) may lead to their solution. By definition, it is the place of the combination of the difference.

Of course, it is not by imitating the past and eighteenth-century ornaments that this will happen. It is also not going to happen by simply commenting through design on the various dislocations and uncertainties of our contemporary condition. I do not believe it is possible, nor that it makes sense, to design buildings that *formally* attempt to blur traditional structures, i.e. that display forms that lie somewhere between abstraction and figuration, or somewhere between structure and ornament, or that are cut up, dislocated for aesthetic reasons. Architecture is not an illustrative art, it does not illustrate theories. (I do not believe you can design deconstruction . . . .) You cannot design a new definition of the city and its architecture. But you may be able to design the conditions that will make it possible for this nonhierarchical, nontraditional society

to happen. By understanding the nature of our contemporary circumstances and the media processes that go with it, architects are in a position to construct conditions that will create a new city and new relationships between spaces and events.

Architecture is not about the conditions of design, but about the design of conditions. Or, to paraphrase Paul Virilio, our object today is not to fulfill the conditions of construction, but to achieve the construction of conditions that will dislocate the most traditional and regressive aspects of our society and simultaneously reorganize these elements in the most liberating way, where our experience becomes the experience of events organized and *strategized* through architecture. Strategy is a key word today in architecture. No more masterplans, no more locating in a fixed place, but a new heterotopia. That is what our cities are striving towards, and here we architects must help them by intensifying the rich collision of events and spaces.

Tokyo and New York only *appear* chaotic; in reality, they mark the appearance of a new urban structure, a new urbanity. Their confrontations and combinations of elements may provide us with the event, the *shock*, that I hope will make the architecture of our cities a *turning-point* in culture and society.

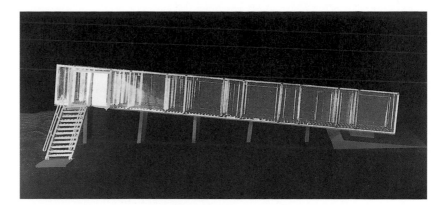

*7. Glass Video
Gallery, Gronin-
gen. Photogram —
elevation, 1990*

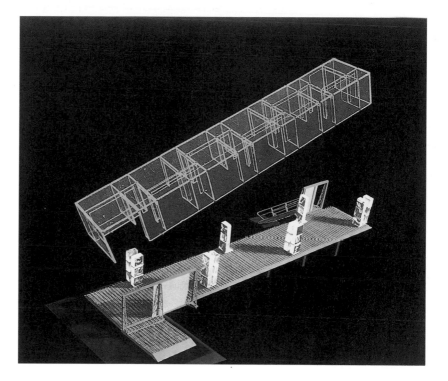

*8. Glass Video
Gallery, Gronin-
gen. Photogram —
exploded view,
1990*

Lebbeus Woods

TERRA NOVA

It's good to be here in Vienna. I want to thank Peter Noever and Regina Haslinger for inviting me and also my friends here who for the past two days have shown me the city.

Tonight, I will divide my remarks into two parts. First, I will speak to you about several ideas that seem important to me and inform my work in particular ways. Then I will show you some of my work, the projects I have initiated or undertaken over the past three years, which form a line of research and development, rising out of the ideas that most interest me.

But before beginning, I want to say that this afternoon I had an amazing experience in the master class of Wolf D. Prix here at the Academy. Some of you who belong to that class are here tonight. For me, it was such a stimulating and powerful experience that, coming into my lecture, I'm not sure whether it was good or bad. It was good, because it made me feel very energetic, but not so good because I realize that now I have to perform on a higher level than usual. But I'm glad for it. I was tremendously excited by the work I saw this afternoon and the spirit of the design studio.

Obviously I'm here to show you my work, because the work itself is ultimately the most important thing and must stand by itself. Yet, as an architect I am concerned not only with making forms, but with thinking, too. The thoughts, the ideas behind the work are very important.

The title I chose for this lecture, *terra nova*, has two meanings for me. The first is "something new." New earth, taken literally, but also something strange. I learned a word when I came to Vienna — *unheimlich*. It refers to something strange, something unknown before, and unfamiliar. When we confront strange, new, unfamiliar things, we are shocked, unsettled. Strangeness makes us come out of our familiar, comfortable ways of thinking and confront a new reality. This is important to me in my work and in my life.

---

1. Solohouse, 1988 – 1989.
Exterior view. Model

The idea of a *terra nova* also refers to a new nature, a type of second nature, which is a *human* nature. Remember how, in the biblical story, Adam and Eve were cast out of the Garden of Eden, out of a wonderful harmony with all of nature. They were cast out because they wanted knowledge. These human beings wanted to judge for themselves what was good, what was evil, what made the world work in its parts and as a whole. So they became separated from nature and went their own way. As a metaphor of our human condition, this is still beautiful, because we remain somehow separate from nature, and because we must also, somehow, reinvent nature for ourselves. We have to *re*-create the world, to inhabit it fully. In this way, all of our utopian schemes are attempts to recreate the Garden, the Eden we lost because we insisted on having knowledge for ourselves. I believe architecture is a supremely important field of work in the attempt to recreate nature and the world, to reinvent our lost paradise, because architecture incorporates so much from all aspects of human experience. The complexity and diversity of human life and thought are, in architecture, transformed into something physical, tangible, something we experience on all levels, from our intellects down to our guts. It is for this reason that I decided to become an architect. With the especially urgent need of the only child to recon-cile himself with the world, I turned to architecture because it seemed to me that by the act of recreation I could achieve this reconciliation. This is perhaps the most important thought that drives my work: to become part of the world, I cannot merely represent it through critique or some kind of mimetic activity, but must invent the world. Not *a* world, not *my* world, but *the* world.

To invent the world, I must include everything in it: everyone in this room, and everyone outside this room; the cities, nature, trees, sky — everything, in all its multiplicity and complexity. I have to do this — it's simply my necessity. But then I believe it's the necessity of all of us today. Throughout the history of Western civilization there has always been a collective mentality we have been able to draw upon to give us an idea of the world and our individual places in it. We've been able to refer to a hierarchy of authority that could tell us the way the world is — kings, scholars, a priesthood. But more and more today we have to find this out for ourselves. We have to be individuals. I think the whole of Western history has to do with putting us in this rather terrible posi-tion. As individuals we have to decide what is right and wrong. We have to decide on our own how to act, whether an action is good or bad. We have to act in such a way that it relates to others, to everything in the world, and not based on a set of rules given to us by authorities, but on our own experiences. In this sense, each of us has the necessity to invent the world, and be responsible for it. This places each of us in a position of tremendous uncertainty, because it's not easy to invent the world, especially when it includes others. Of course, architects have to do this all the time.

It is our modern fate to live in uncertainty and ambiguity. We inhabit space in which we're not sure exactly how to move. Then how do we do this? No one can tell. Today, no one can tell you how to act, to think, to be. That's why I liked the master class of Wolf Prix that I visited today — because everyone was struggling to find his/her own way of dealing with reality through direct experience of conditions. I'm older than these students, but I am still a student, trying to learn and develop my way of seeing the world through the making of architecture.

With all I've said, I want to make one thing very clear: it's not for me to tell others how to live. As an architect, as an individual, I can only speak for myself. I stand here and speak only for myself. I can't instruct you how to behave or how to act. That is part of our ambiguity and uncertainty. But we can have a conversation, a dialogue. We can exchange feelings, thoughts, ideas. We can each make works and assert them in a forum, whether it's a class in an academy, the streets of a city, in magazines, museums, wherever it may happen. We can have this dialogue if we choose to, and through it I believe we will find our way to some kind of community again. Even though it's not clear what that community may be, even though we can no longer live according to traditions or the old ways of collective thinking, a new kind of community and city is possible through free exchange and dialogue. I'm glad to say that there is a growing number of architects willing to take on the ambiguity and uncertainty of our present situation.

How, then, does an architect deal with this situation? Through space and form. What kind of space, what kind of form? Well, that's yet to be seen. However, it is clear now that architects must look at ways to organize space that differ radically from the classical ways that served the past. We know those ways, and they worked for a different, collective way of thinking and living, but now we're on our ground, and we must find our own way. I believe a new kind of architecture and human community will evolve.

The most direct way for architects to have a dialogue among themselves and with others is through building. I raise this subject because building is obviously a great issue in architecture. It is important to build — and, clearly, architecture is about construction. But I think it's also possible to engage in a dialogue of architecture through drawings and models and other means — even through writing. I prefer the visual. Ideas that can be embodied in words are somehow parallel to

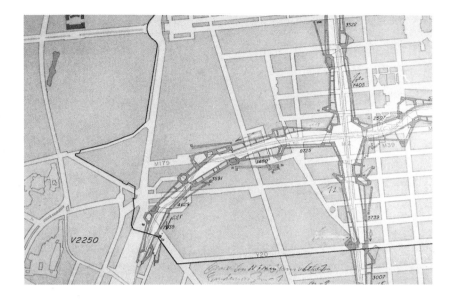

2. Underground Berlin, 1988. Composite plan near the city center

those embodied in visual form. Still, what matters ultimately is that we create the energy of dialogue. We put it out in whatever form we can. If we don't have a client for a building, then we make architecture any way we can. We assert it. We make some drawings. We put it forward.

On this point, some people ask me, "Are you serious? Do you want to build this work that you draw?" I say, "Yes, I would like to build. I would like the test of building, because I think it's the greatest test. But in my drawings I've already built." For me and, hopefully, for you, these works exist and are real. They are built, constructed. They are material and no longer purely in the realm of the mind. They have physical form and are tangible. The important thing is to make your architecture in whatever way you can, and let the rest of the world take care of itself. Having said these things, I would like to show you several of my projects.

Over the years I have initiated many of my own projects. But several of my best projects, those from the past three years that I will show tonight, have come as a result of an invitation to make a proposal, much the way all architects work. In 1988, Kristin Feireiss, who has organized many exhibitions of architecture in Europe and runs the Aedes Gallery in Berlin, invited a number of architects to make proposals for Berlin in response to the question "Berlin: Denkmal oder Denkmodell?"

We know, of course, what has happened in Berlin since 1988, but at that time The Wall was still very much in evidence. Being an American, I was fascinated by The Wall, by the idea of the political division of the city — even though West Berliners seemed to ignore it. This particular map (fig. 2), which is a composite, shows the Tiergarten, the center of

Berlin, the Friedrichstrasse, Checkpoint Charlie, the Cultural Center ...
When I was first in Berlin, I learned that the U-Bahn lines still ran
beneath The Wall, that the trains ran from West Berlin, through the East
and back again — they simply didn't stop in East Berlin. It seemed to
me that if the people of Berlin were ever to reunite their city, they would
do it themselves, regardless of the governments involved. I proposed that
they would do it underground and they would use the underground
spaces of the U-Bahn that existed, represented by the yellow line on the
map, constructing a series of larger underground spaces beneath it,
represented by the configurations below the street patterns.

In the section (fig. 3) you can see the street level of the Friedrichstrasse, the U-Bahn lines below, and below these the underground spaces
I proposed, the civic spaces of an underground community. Within each
civic space the people from the West and the East would secretly begin
to build structures — a new Berlin community. Since the datum of the
city is at the level of the street above, they would build their structures
from the street downward, so they would create an inverted city of
inverted towers.

These inverted towers (fig. 4) would be constructed for both living
and work, of necessity very compact and concentrated. One promise of
my projects is that I am not only interested in an architecture that serves
an existing idea of living, but more so in the prospect of new ways
of living — much as when I earlier said that the strange, the new
introduces us through shock to a new, deeply personal conception of
what the world is. So it seemed to me that even more important than
the political aspect of this project, which was its initial premise, was a
set of new conditions of living: those found underground, in the earth,
where previously we put only trains, or — even more commonly — the

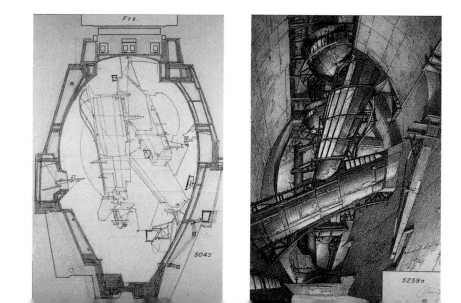

3. *Underground
Berlin, 1988.
Section: civic space
with inverted
towers*

4. *Underground
Berlin, 1988. Civic
space with inverted
tower and bridge*

dead. But here we would build a new kind of community, of structures built from the upper levels downward, or bridging across the civic space, forming the basis of a new way of life.

A new way of life — what is it? Well, all our ways of living are connected with the physical conditions of the world we inhabit, including those underground. Here there's an entirely new climate of physical forces — seismic, gravitational, electromagnetic forces that are active within the entire planetary mass of the earth. The way of life I imagined — or actually proposed — was meant in some way to respond to this underground climate of physical conditions and forces. The architecture, the structures are composed of thin metal sheets, separated from each other by delicate instruments or materials that would allow their inhabitants to sense the subtle and delicate forces animate in the earth. The structures are almost like instruments themselves, musical instruments, in the sense that they move harmoniously with geo-mechanical and geomagnetic forces of precise frequencies. These may not be heard, not even always felt, but on the level of thought and its electromagnetic reality, a harmony with the earth and the present instant is achieved through the instrumentation of the architecture. The entire network of interconnected structures resonates as an ensemble, an urban unit.

Each of these structures is a living-laboratory, a laboratory for experimental living, for living existentially in the moment. What are we doing? Why do we do anything? Why do we get up in the morning and do what we do? These are questions I always ask. In the underground

5. Underground Berlin, 1988. Alexanderplatz, projection tower. Model

6. Underground Berlin, 1988. Alexanderplatz, projection tower

city, the purpose of living is found in living fully in the present, in the Now, in harmony with precise but changing physical conditions. I mean this not in a spiritual or metaphysical way — I don't know about those things. All I know is what I feel, what I taste and touch. This is an architecture of sensuality, if you will, its an architecture of materiality, an architecture one feels.

Drawing is for me a way of entering into architectural space and form and into thoughts. But models are important, too. Each stage in the development of architecture is a test of the former stages. So, in the Underground Berlin project, the models were made to test the ideas embodied in the drawings. Even in cardboard and wood, they achieve a stage beyond the drawings, which investigate the tectonics and spaces in greater detail.

In making the proposition for an underground city and the way of life growing out of a new climate of physical conditions, I recognized that its inhabitants would one day want to return to the surface of the earth from which they came. They would not be happy to live below forever. I proposed that they would not return to the surface in a passive way, as they would want to bring with them what they had learned from their experiences below. In the underground civic spaces they would build towers (fig. 5) that would one day break the datum of the surface of the earth and the city above. I call these "projection towers." They project the idea, the energy of re-emergence, but also physical things — a human energy, and also the energy of the idea of physicality, of the Now, of the tenuousness of construction and the sensing of the delicate yet powerful forces active in the earth. The models were an investigation of the idea of a projection tower, which is a single shaft, upon which are constructed other elements. What is being projected, then, is not simply the elements of the tower itself, but elements that are meant to separate from the tower, to leave the tower and go beyond it. The central shaft becomes the staging shaft for the construction of smaller elements that are built in order to leave, to go out into the wider world. In this drawing (fig. 6) I attempted to show what that projection would be. From the tower, these elements, fragments, would be cast, projected — I didn't know how or why. They are simply like seeds, spores, the generative elements of a new culture of physicality sent into the world.

That was in 1988. I had taken the project as far as I could at that time. The following year, Kristin Feireiss — one of my best clients — said, "Well, now we'll do some projects for Paris." I said, "Great — this is what I've been waiting for." This, she said, would mean a proposal for the city of Paris at the beginning of the twenty-first Century: "Paris: Architecture et Utopia."

Well, it was quite natural for me to think of my Berlin project, and the last memory I had of Berlin was of these elements that were flying off into the air, to some unknown destination. And so I said to myself, "Of course — they're going to Paris." And what will happen over Paris is that they will collect in the sky over the city. Berlin is a city of the North. It is a city of interiors, underground and above. But Paris is more a city of the South, a city of light and air — they have the Paris Air Show every year. In this way my project became "Aerial Paris."

The fragments, the tectonic elements of the Berlin project, born of a culture of the earth, were brought together and joined to form a project over Paris. It was an entirely experimental idea: when I began, I didn't know how it would end. I began to explore the synthesis of these fragments, then to imagine structures, aerial structures formed of these shards of materials. I also imagined the tectonic that would come from joining these parts together. How would the bent surfaces be made and how would they be connected together? And how would they relate to the earth below? In my earliest drawings, these cables just went off the edge of the drawing to somewhere. But that was all right, that was enough to begin. I felt there was a tie to the earth. I kept working, because this seemed like an intriguing idea.

Being a very practical person, I asked myself: "Well, what's holding these in the air? How can these be in the air? For thousands of years people dreamt of flying, but they couldn't. Now they've invented aircraft engines. But these aerial structures are floating — no engines. How can it be done?" So I began to form the concept of "magnetic lift." The earth, as we know, is surrounded by a powerful magnetic field, which is really an electrical field. If one were to create within it a form, a heavy object, charged with a corresponding electrical field, one would have a form of magnetic attraction. In the air, the structures I proposed would become a dipolar magnet and would use the ambient magnetic fields of the earth in which to rise. This would happen in much the same way as the little pellet of superconducting material the media showed us several years ago was maintained in the air above an electrical field. It has been done. So I seized on this idea and projected a new technology. I think it's quite natural for architects to propose, to drive technology. Engineers can work out the mathematics, but we should make the proposition, and not simply say, "What does technology tell us?" We architects should tell technology. So I've sent out the word on flying.

As I began to develop these aerial structures, I was very interested in the typical architectural concerns of construction, but also in form and space. Because I work mostly alone, drawing for me is a way to shape, to form, to construct. In my opening comments I said, "Well, I'm

7. Aerial Paris, 1989. Aeroliving labs with nets. Heterarchy

8. Aerial Paris, 1989. Magnetic vortex at the Eiffel Tower

building." So I am building in my drawings, I'm building using the detailed manner that I have developed: I'm interested in the connection of parts, in the nature of surfaces, in the exact way elements come together. My drawings are investigations of architecture on many levels.

As I developed this series of aerial structures I realized that each one is different from the others, each one is unique and individual. Michael Sorkin calls one of them (fig. 7) "Boxy-moron" which is perfect. It's about the contradictions in the combination of simple Euclidean geometry with something stranger and more ambiguous. I like his comment, because he understood perfectly what this relationship is about.

As I looked at the various aerial structures I began to think about what kind of ensemble they would make — what kind of community? Clearly, they are free-wheeling structures, they're kinetic, moving in the fluid of the atmosphere. While studying the landscape of Paris, I looked at the Eiffel Tower and said: "Now this is a great piece of iron, and iron distorts electromagnetic fields, creating a kind of vortex above the tower." Here (fig. 8) the aerial structures combine with a new element: the nets that twist, not only in the wind, but also in the magnetic vortex that circles the tower. In other parts of Paris, the lack of magnetic distortions results in a smoother flow of structures and nets, more laterally, more horizontally. But in any case the nets had now become part of the aerial ensemble and are pulled by the heavy structures across the sky. In this city plan of Paris, there is a continuous stream of instants when the nets form a new type of grid, a new type of urban pattern, which becomes the key to a new kind of community that is being formed and re-formed over the city.

I say a new city, a new community. What kind of community can be created by free-floating structures, whose locations are fixed? Their inhabitants are like gypsies, or like people living in automobiles. What type of ensemble could they make? I made a series of drawings exploring various changing patterns, groupings that seemed to be temporary, without a center, without any sort of hierarchy or fixed order. Each drawing is one instant in an endless sequence of shiftings and changings. At a certain moment, I realized finally what sort of community this was, what the program for my project had become.

It was a circus, an aerial circus, created by a group of individuals who become very proficient at living in the changing atmosphere of the sky and perform as individuals, but come together freely in various temporary arrangements, somewhat unpredictably. Their ensemble of forms and performances is without predetermined composition, without any classical order, without center, or hierarchy or symmetry. Looking very closely at any momentary ensemble, the same principle holds true for their interconnection, and for the diverse elements within each structure. Each drawing I've made shows a moment, only an instant in the continuous shifting of structures, in response to individual moves and unpredictable aerial conditions.

Now, to prove that I am an engineer, I will explain how the individual aerial structures receive their electricity to generate the dipolar fields by which they stay aloft. One aspect of these great nets is that, as they are dragged through the air, there's a tremendous build-up in them of static electricity as well as electricity acquired by sheer movement through the earth's magnetic field. The cables seen in the drawings emerging from the structures to "somewhere" connect the nets to the aerial structures, transferring the electrical energy continuously being generated to the structures. Hence — in the manner I explained — they fly.

The architecture of the nets is perhaps more interesting. Today, in the master class, we saw interesting projects that had to do with the temporariness of form. In drawings which I made in an exuberance for these nets, I explored their twistings and turnings, the idea of an architecture that defines and organizes space, but always in a changing and unexpected way.

There are many more drawings of this project. Each explores the possibilities of joining in diverse ways elements which are themselves unique, seeking an unpredictable architecture, something kinetic and elusive, but material and always part of an aerial world. The time came when I decided to test drawn ideas and architecture further, by building one of the aerial structures.

What began as a model ended up as a one-to-one scale construction (fig. 9). Beginning with a fairly traditional working drawing, I and some young colleagues — who are strong and energetic — began to build one of these structures in a Brooklyn workshop. When it was finished, it was some four meters long and quite heavy, yet delicate. Shipping it to Paris was not easy, but we did it. When it arrived at the Pavillion de L'Arsenal there was some shock and consternation among the museum staff, but eventually we were able to convince them this was "architecture" — an amazing achievement in itself. And so they paid the large shipping bill, which was the most important part. Then they hired — it was totally extraordinary, because they didn't trust us to hang it in the high space — they hired mountain climbers to climb up the big trusses and hang it with mountain ropes. That was a little clumsy, but okay.

Of course, this aerial structure doesn't fly in a magnetic field. I know that, I accept that. But as I said, the technology is proposed. Now the engineers just have to find a way, and I'm sure they will.

The interior space of the structure was not fully developed, because the construction focused more on materials — sheet steel, wood, cable, tubing — than on representation. It became an experiment in tectonics and form more than a full-bodied architecture. Yet it's not without interest in that regard. For example, it achieves in the assemblage of elements the diversity I always want to find in my work, the differences between the reflective and the dull, between the very thin and the massive, between the very tense and the more relaxed and serene, between things that move, like this flap, and things that move very differently, like the broad sheets of steel.

This construction reveals another aspect of architecture that the next project deals with more directly. I've talked about geometry, ideas of community, tectonics, but not yet about light.

I want to confess this to you — light is the thing that makes me want to live. To see light is my greatest pleasure, my *raison d'être*. Yet light is a curious thing. Space is filled with light, but we can only see light when it is reflected from something else. The slide projector in this room casts a beam of light that is visible only because it's reflected from humidity, water vapor, cigarette smoke and whatever else is in the air.

Last year I decided to make a series of light-measuring instruments, which I call "light-metrical" instruments. They are constructions using simple materials — steel and copper wires and sheets — whose purpose is to reflect light and to measure it. By measurement I mean that only when we define a precise shape that reflects light do we bring light out of a state of darkness and chaos into a measurable state of experience. By making forms and surfaces of precise dimensions, we interact with

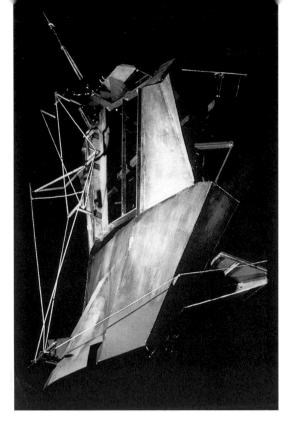

9. Aerial Paris,
1989. Geomagnetic
aeroliving lab.
Model

light by giving it structure, by ordering it not only in a spatial sense, but also with respect to intensity, color, and character. The very materials we use present light to us in precise frequencies — harmonious, dissonant, strong or weak.

By using actual materials, rather than those simulated by drawing, one can study the precise nature of light in reflectance. Sometimes people have said, "Well, your drawings and constructions always seem to be decaying. You must be a decadent Romantic, who likes to think about decay and death." But I don't think about decay as anything but an enrichment of form, an animation of surfaces. The steel sheet, for example, in its naked state is contrasted with very precise painted areas, or areas of surface that are weathered and peeling, broken, or have fallen away, the whole revealing a variation not only of shapes, but of different frequencies, colors, intensities of reflected light. These are objects of pleasure and of thought, a primal architecture and landscape of light.

I want to show you two more projects. The first is a project I finished only ten days ago and have included in my lecture because it completes a trilogy of projects that began in Berlin in 1988, moved to Paris in 1989, and now concludes, back in Berlin. Just two months ago an invitation was made to a number of architects to make proposals for what has been called "the new Berlin," the reunified Berlin, Berlin without The Wall.

Now that the whole city can celebrate its traditional center, what will be built there? I knew there were many famous und wonderful architects making projects in response to this invitation, and I also wanted to make a contribution, to participate in this dialogue, because I feel very deeply about Berlin.

I realized immediately that my work of the past three years had been developing toward something non-monumental. In my Underground Berlin and Aerial Paris projects there were monumental structures, in terms of scale, but in these projects I was not interested in monumentalizing established institutions of culture — ministries, corporate headquarters, museums, business and commercial operations — but instead in exploring new possibilities of urban life and human experience. The thought that the centers of the old European capitals will one by one become cultural theme parks for tourism is anathema to me.

I began to work by making collages of aerial photographic maps of the center of Berlin and abstractions of structures that are arriving over Berlin, perhaps from Paris, perhaps from some undefined region of thought or instinct. They express no purpose whatsoever and resemble the light-metrical instruments or the aerial Paris structures. No definite scale has been established.

These ambiguous elements arrive over Berlin, characteristically — according to the experimental way I work — without much idea of what their purpose is or what would happen next. I began to interpret them as composite structures — similar in spirit and construction to those for Paris — but with some differences. For one thing, they exist in an abstract space. There are no sky and clouds, no atmosphere per se, but only a mathematical domain. Also, there are new types of elements, crushed or wrinkled surfaces as well as the already familiar singly and

10. Berlin Free-Zone, 1990.
Free-space sections

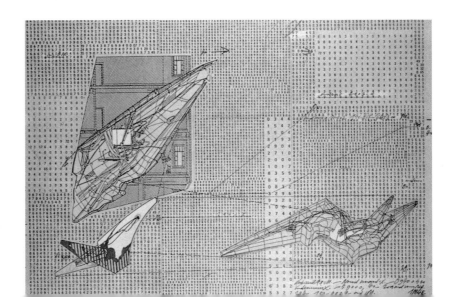

11. Berlin Free-Zone, 1990. Free-space section

doubly curved ones. I haven't mentioned yet that in my projects I am very interested in structures that derive their strength from their shape, such as one finds in aircraft of all kinds. One doesn't need columns and beams and slabs, or any kind of skeleton — in fact, in a kinetic architecture one doesn't want that type of rectilinear structure at all. If one takes a sheet of paper and crumples it, it acquires great structural strength, relatively speaking. The same with a sheet of steel.

At first, these bent and curved forms didn't seem to belong in the center of Berlin, but then I began to realize that, yes, they did belong, as something unknown, undefined, uncertain, ambiguous, having to do with a potential in the city yet to be realized. So I proposed that these structures should enter existing structures, the already known fabric of the city, and become a hidden city, of entirely unknown purpose or meaning.

The development of this proposition can be seen in fig. 10. The metaphorical entity is understood as a three-dimensional structure composed of two surfaces, each partly Euclidean and deterministic — a cone, a cylinder, unbroken planes — and partly broken, bent, crushed, of indeterminate geometry. Within the space created between the two surfaces, certain points of focus are established and connected. Now when this assembly appears in the Cartesian frame of an existing building, it becomes entirely interior. In the section drawing (fig. 11) one sees clearly the existing spaces, the inserted spaces and within these, the points or nodes — places of rest in the active spaces. They are not easy spaces to be in, so there need to be places within to sit or work, to lie down, sleep. These could also be stations, nodes where telecommunications equipment could be — a computer, telephone, a fax machine — to make contact with other spaces in the city. There could be instruments that we don't know yet, that would measure light, or the vibrations from cars passing on the streets.

I call these spaces "free-spaces." They are not free in the sense that they are neutral or interchangeable, rather they provide a freedom that can only come from something very particular, very precise, definite, and unique, a unique configuration of space, shape and texture of surface, a precise frequency of light, the certain angle between surfaces. It's not a Cartesian world of neutrality, but, physically, something very definite. Beyond the precise physical conditions, the existential conditions of a given moment, these spaces are undefined.

Two criteria have emerged from the work thus far. The first, and perhaps most important: the free-spaces are without any predetermined use. They are useless spaces.

The second criterion of free-spaces is that they are difficult to occupy, so anyone who would want to occupy, live, work or act in the space, would have to invent a way from the physical conditions at hand, not relying on existing preconceptions or conventions. There would be resting points, platforms, a curtain or blanket to draw around oneself to rest in this difficult zone, this free-zone. Real freedom is difficult, right? There's nothing left to lose.

Returning to the cityplan (fig. 12) and my interest in patterns of community, what then is this new pattern of living within the city? Well, the black figures are free-spaces within existing buildings, connected by changing lines of communications, invisible electronic paths. Thus, a new community can be established at the center of Berlin, a network of thought and action established by free individuals. Of course, the outcome of all this is uncertain, but a new potential is created, for the city and its inhabitants. It is up to them what they do with it.

12. Berlin Free-Zone, 1990. Free-space network: new Berlin Center

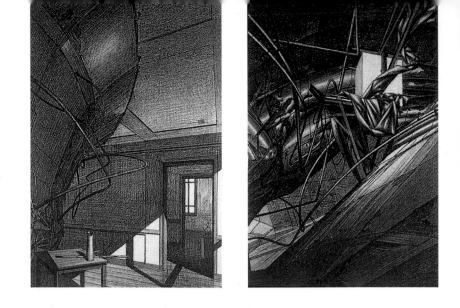

13. Berlin Free-Zone, 1990. Exterior view of free-space

14. Berlin Free-Zone, 1990. Free-space interior

My way of working becomes clear here. I make a series of perspective drawings, very quickly — I don't spend much time, because the drawing is only a way to study, to enter into precise physical conditions of light, space, surface, materials. Then I make more analytical drawings, including "case studies" of existing buildings, where I am able to analyze free-spaces within existing ones, using orthographic tools of investigation. Horizontal and vertical sectional drawings are still useful in the investigation of complex, non-Euclidean geometries — they in no way diminish the effort to invent these new and indeterminate, more difficult geometries — but only bring together two ways of making space and form together. The result: more difficulties and complexities, of a different order. Where the enclosure of free-space meets the interior of the Cartesian room, the only external presence of free-space, the space of the new and hidden city within a city, is revealed (fig. 13). Two worlds have been made, and co-exist. I could have used glass or more diaphanous materials in the free-space construction, but I did not, because they are very separate, worlds apart. When you are in the free-zone (fig. 14), maybe on the platform, leaning back on its sloping surface, confronting the electronic instruments, or pulling the cloth around you for warmth, you exist completely within its precise conditions, and no longer belong to that abstraction, the city of Berlin. That is the nature of freedom, the price it requires.

Because many of my ideas and work have been connected with large-scale concerns, cities and communities and complexes of diverse structures, I always return to the single, isolated structure. Can I make one structure that embodies the crucial ideas? Am I relying too much on a large-scale project to make the architecture I want to make? The

Solohouse made in 1989 was a test, and in a way, a critique of earlier projects, including those for Paris and Berlin.

The Solohouse is a house, a basic unit of habitation, for one individual (fig. 15). It has one space, which is not really divided, but only modulated by a series of intervening leaves or platforms within the space. The plan reveals the same structural idea that appears in many of the earlier projects. The structural rigidity derives from the form itself. It's really stress-skin, aircraft construction. No skeleton is needed.

As ever, perspective drawings came first, as a means of seeing the architecture as part of a total landscape, a world. It's unfortunate that all the tentative, exploratory stages of these drawings are not visible in the final result, which is elaborated to define as much of the architecture as possible. But many experiments are involved and there are variations even between the finished drawings. I feel no obligation to make them agree with each other. If I were making drawings for workmen to build from, I might do otherwise; but these have a different purpose, the purpose of invention. Each defines a set of variations on shape, proportion, materials, elements. I feel very free with them. They are mine and serve my purposes.

The form of the house is so unitary, so compact, that it had to be broken so light could enter — there are fissures where it breaks into the

15. Solohouse,
1988 – 1989.
Exterior study

interior of the house and from which, once inside, certain views to the outside are possible. I always think of Corbusier's Villa Savoie — the views outward are discrete, very selected. The intention is not to control viewing, but to make it something definite, something unique.

A friend commented on this interior drawing (fig. 16): "Well, this seems so domestic!" And it *is* cheerful — there's a little chair, and a drawing pad, and a drapery and, well, I don't know, I guess the pet, the housepet. At this point I realized I had to break out. I had to do something else. So, naturally, I made the model (fig. 1), a very ambitious model. It was shown in Frankfurt last year, in the "Künstlerhäuser" exhibition. It's a large steel model, but I couldn't quite fit inside. If I can find someone to provide the necesssary funding, maybe we can build it large enough to be in. But never mind, I don't care. We built a steel model.

When a model is built, certain things happen. When you make drawings it's one thing, but when you make models it's something else. When you make buildings it's something else again. I think the architect always has to be prepared for the transformations, and his architecture should be such that it gains from them. I think the Solohouse has.

One transformation was from copper-coated steel, which in the drawings made the surfaces polychromatic, to raw steel — much tougher. The model revealed that coated steel was too soft, the polychrome too pretty, not hard enough for this shell. There are the openings for entrance and for light, incised as before, but new elements have appeared. At the forward edge, there is an instrument, perhaps a light-metrical instrument that you may recall from earlier projects. Or maybe it has another purpose, one that we can invent for it. Maybe it's an instrument for examining the air around the house, maybe one that looks back into the surface of the house at its minute changes, its molecular structure. Or maybe it's a place where the inhabitant can interact with a series of light changes and material conditions.

In the model I am able to explore more precisely than in drawings the nature of the materials at hand. Materials are what we deal with. We are materialists, we architects — the most terrible and passionate materialists. We see in the nature of construction how things relate, interact, are joined: the welded seams, the wood supports pinned to the little airplane flap over the entrance. Each of the tectonic elements exists and comes together with the others in a particular and unique way. The surfaces are weathered, and become like no other surfaces in the world. This is what fascinates me about architecture, and about living — the diversity, the complexity, the multiplicity, the individuality, the differences of one thing, one moment, from all others.

Looking up the sloping plane on which the forward point of the house is pressed, we see the entrance. It is not reached head-on, but along a ledge to the guarded door. Behind it rises the interior, the solo-space of the house. Illuminated within, one can see past the ledge, through the grilled door, to the platforms above, and the ladder by which one reaches them (fig. 17). Up there is yet another instrument, a light-metrical or electromagnetic one, with a high steel wand for webbing together invisible but quite tangible forces, or simply for catching the light in a certain way — or, perhaps, for sending out signals into the space of night beyond, to other solohouses, other remote places in the world. Here there is also a steel chair for the lone inhabitant, and a screen for viewing outward or perhaps a mirror for looking back at himself. In the end it's the same thing.

From a distance, in the darkness, we see the house illuminated from within. I should speak somehow about that condition I opened with, the existential condition of isolation we moderns are privileged to experience. The future is uncertain, and the meaning of all this is hopelessly ambiguous, yet we are placed by these very conditions fully in the richness and power of the present moment.

Philip Johnson

EPILOGUE

The architects who here present their work are arguably among the leading practitioners in the world. Most of them we exhibited at the Museum of Modern Art in New York in 1988 under the rubric "Deconstructivists." Only Jean Nouvel, the architect of the beautiful Institut Ardbe in Paris, is a doubtful candidate for this label: his work has the order and the clarity of French tradition.

The most verbal of the present company is naturally enough Peter Eisenman. He persuasively propounds the "theory that there is no theory" of the French intellectual: "At last we are through with objective truths. Truth, of course, must be used as a concept in our living, but it does not exist" (my paraphrase). The nonrational, the emotional, the nonlogical motivation of Eisenman's shapes, sizes, colors, details is evident in his work.

Coop Himmelblau with their "brennende Architektur," their creative flames, make buildings with sloping beams, X-shaped vertical supports, interpenetrating thrusting shapes, "dancing chimneys."

Daniel Libeskind talks about a voided void, "a void which has itself been voided" — a deconstruction which has itself been deconstructed. The precarious slanted mass of his Berlin housing, propped upon drunken columns, and his zigzag, bolt-of-lightning museum are "splintered" monuments in today's mad world.

The most daring, romantic intellectual of all the group is Zaha Hadid. Her beams fly, her curves intersect, her façades lean out. In the theoretical part of her account she makes clear the ancestry of her shapes: Malevich and the Russian avantgarde of the twenties. She is most clearly of all the grandchild of that great modern movement. Zaha, however, is no epigone; she is an original.

Lebbeus Woods is our true dreamer, artist, ideologue of the young. He does not build, but his beautiful drawings are more moving and provocative than many a built structure. Every movement must have its prophets, its seers.

California as always marches to a different drummer: Thom Mayne and his partner, Michael Rotondi, are representative of the Young Turks of that precocious culture. There is no connection here with Malevich or the Constructivists. Mayne and Rotondi's roots hardly go back before their slightly older Californian guru, Frank Gehry.

These Californians have shown a new concern about what connects what and how: column to base, column to beam, tension bar to socket — an interest lacking up to now. This might be labeled a decorative use of connections, a jewelry of joinery. It is more. Their own credo best expresses what they are doing, and not coincidentally it expresses what most of this extraordinary group of architects are aiming at: "Our interest is in an architecture composed of a series of independent but connected pieces, and in spaces housing simple functions that have been pushed, distorted or aggrandized." The result of this interest is an almost Arts and Crafts approach to structural members, an attitude more reminiscent of Frank Lloyd Wright than of Le Corbusier, more Scarpa than Neutra.

The ultimate aim of all architects is surely beauty (a word hopelessly out of fashion today); these architects, I feel, share that aim. But right now their work appears as something upsetting and disturbing: exciting forms that are antistructural, nonrational, antiregular, nonmodular. We live in a slippery (meaningless) world where certainty is not even desired, much less attainable.

Mies would turn over in his grave. Malevich and Rodchenko would understand (they ought to — many of the slanted, crossing beams came from them). Plato would not understand but Heraclitus certainly would — Descartes and Bertrand Russell would not, Karl Kraus and Dostoevski would.

This is a world in which neither the rules of Beaux Arts or the Bauhaus on the one hand nor the functional socialist rules of the Modern control our destinies. We are on our own.

The wave of the future in architecture is, of course, unknowable, but these artists, in my opinion, represent the wave of today.

ALOIS MÜLLER

Alois Müller is a writer and curator at the Museum of Design in Zurich. He regularly publishes articles on art and architecture in journals and newspapers, organizes exhibitions, and lectures at the philosophy and art history seminars of the University of Zurich.

COOP HIMMELBLAU

Coop Himmelblau was founded in 1968 in Vienna by Wolf D. Prix (born in Vienna in 1942) and Helmut Swiczinsky (born in Poznan, Poland, in 1944). In 1989 the two architects opened a second office in Los Angeles (in the same year building started on the Open House, also in California). Their recently realized projects include the Funder factory in St. Veit/Glan, Kärnten, and the attic conversion in Falkestrasse, Vienna. In 1987 Coop Himmelblau won two major competitions: the international urban design competition for Melun-Sénart, a satellite town south of Paris, and the competition for the conversion of the Ronacher Theater in Vienna. They have shown their work at many international exhibitions, including the exhibition "Deconstructivist Architecture" at the Museum of Modern Art in New York (1988), and have lectured or taught as visiting professors at universities in Europe, Japan, Australia and the United States. They live and work in Vienna and Los Angeles.

PETER EISENMAN

Peter Eisenman was born in 1932 in Newark, New Jersey. He studied architecture at Cornell University, Ithaca, NY (1951 – 55), at Columbia University, New York (1959 – 60) and at Cambridge University, England (1960 – 63). He has taught at Princeton University and since 1975 at the Cooper Union, New York. He edited the architecture journal *Oppositions* (1973 – 82) and was first director of the Institute for Architecture and Urban Studies, New York (1967 – 82). He has participated in numerous exhibitions, including "40 under 40" at the Architectural League, New York (1966), "The New City: Architecture and Urban Renewal" at the Museum of Modern Art, New York (1967), "Architecture of Museums" at the Museum of Modern Art, New York (1973), and "Deconstructivist Architecture" at the Museum of Modern Art, New York (1988). His built projects include The Manhattan Waterfront, New York (1966) and the University of California Arts Center, Berkeley (1965), with Michael Graves. Recent projects have included the Wexner Center at Ohio State University (1989). Peter Eisenman lives and works in New York.

ZAHA HADID

Born in 1950 in Baghdad, Iraq, Zaha Hadid studied architecture at the Architectural Association School of Architecture in London (1972 – 77) under Leon Krier, Jeremy Dixon and Rem Kohlhaas. From 1976 to 1978 she was a member of the OMA group (Office for Metropolitan Architecture), and subsequently opened her own office in London. She taught at the Architectural Association from 1977 to 1986, at Harvard University, Cambridge (1986) and at Columbia University, New York (1987). Zaha Hadid won first prize in the international competition for The Peak in Hong Kong (1983). Numerous group and one-woman shows have included "Deconstructivist Architecture" at the Museum of Modern Art, New York (1988) and the Max Protetch Group Show, New York (1989). Zaha Hadid lives and works in London.

DANIEL LIBESKIND

Daniel Libeskind was born in 1946 in Poland and studied musicology in Israel, architecture at the Cooper Union in New York (under John Hejduk), and architectural history and theory at Essex University in England. He has taught at universities in North America, Europe, Japan and Scandinavia. He was founder and director of the Architecture Intermundium in Milan (1986 – 89), and was senior scholar at the Center for Humanities, Paul Getty Foundation. In 1987 he won the IBA competition with the design of the City Edge, and in 1989 was awarded first prize in the international competition for the design of the Extension to the Berlin Museum incorporating a Jewish Museum. Since then he has lived and worked in Berlin. Other projects have included a permanent pavilion for the World's Greenery Fair in Osaka, Japan (1990) and a villa in Berlin (1990). He has taken part in numerous exhibitions in Europe, Japan and the United States (including the exhibition "Deconstructivist Architecture" at the Museum of Modern Art, New York, in 1988) and received many awards, from the National Endowment for the Arts, the Graham Foundation, and other bodies.

MORPHOSIS

The group Morphosis was set up by
Thom Mayne and Michel Rotondi in 1974.
Both grew up in Southern California and
studied at the University of Southern
California; Thom Mayne then went on
to the Graduate School of Design in
Harvard. They have been teaching since
the seventies at the South California
Institute of Architecture, of which Thom
Mayne was one of the founders. Morphosis
have won awards for several of their
projects, including the National AIA Award
(1988) and the Progressive Architecture
Award (1985/87/88/89). In the eighties the
group built striking restaurants (the best
known is Kate Mantilini in Los Angeles,
1986) and business premises (such as the
Vecta International furniture store in 1988
and the Leon Maxe ladies' fashion store,
also in 1988). They have built private
houses (Sixth Street House, 1987; Crawford
Residence, 1988), offices (Higoshi Azabu
Tower in Tokyo, 1989) and public buildings,
including the Comprehensive Cancer Clinic
in Los Angeles, 1987, with its highly complex
technical and psychological concept. With
their architecture of metamorphoses and
transformations, Morphosis is now, along
with Frank Gehry, among the best-known
exponents of the new architecture in California. Rotondi left Morphosis in 1991.

JEAN NOUVEL

Jean Nouvel was born in 1945 in Fumel,
France. He studied architecture at the
Ecole des Beaux Arts in Paris (ENSBA
diploma in 1971). He was co-founder of the
French architects' group "Mars 1976" and
one of the organizers of the international
advisory body for the planning of the
Quartier des Halles in Paris (1979). He
organized the first architecture biennial
at the Centre Pompidou in Paris in 1980.
He has entered numerous architectural
competitions (including the prize-wining
project for an opera-house in Tokyo in
1987, together with Philippe Starck).
Projects realized include the documentation
center for CNRS in Nancy (1989), the
redesign of the art gallery Quai Voltaire
(1989), the renovation for the theater in
Belfort (1983), and the Institut du Monde
Arabe in Paris in 1987. Jean Nouvel lives
and works in Paris.

MICHAEL SORKIN

Michael Sorkin was born in Washington,
DC, and studied architecture at Harvard
and at the Massachusetts Institute of
Technology in Cambridge. He has taught
architecture and urban design at the
Cooper Union, Columbia University, and
Yale University. His work includes practical and research-related projects, such as
Los Olivos (a park in Mexico City), a series
of Animal Houses, Model Cities (as study
of utopian urban models), and several
designs for large buildings, including the
Hanseatic Skyscrapers. His work has
recently been exhibited at the Artist's
Space Gallery, New York, and the Aedes
Galerie, Berlin. For ten years he was
architecture critic for the *Village Voice*
in New York. Two books by Sorkin will
shortly be published, *Exquisite Corpse*,
a collection of his architectural reviews,
and *Variations on a Theme Park*, essays on
contemporary American urbanism. Michael
Sorkin lives and works in New York.

LEBBEUS WOODS

Lebbeus Woods was born in 1940 in Lansing, Michigan; he studied at the Purdue University School of Engineering and the University of Illinois School of Architecture. His intensive preoccupation with architectural theory is evidenced by a wide range of publications, such as *Architecture, Sculpture, Painting Series* (1979), *Einstein Tomb* (1980), AEON: The Architecture of Time (1982), and by lectures in America and Europe (Architectural Association, London; Städel School, Frankfurt; Massachusetts Institute of Technology). ebbeus Woods has also had many one-man and group shows, inluding "Origins" (Architectural Association, London, 1985), "Centricity" (AEDES Galerie, Berlin, 1987), "Terra Nova" (Fenster Galerie für Architektur, Frankfurt), "Vision der Moderne" (1986) and "Künstlerhäuser" (1989) at the German Architecture Museum, Frankfurt. In 1988 Lebbeus Woods and Olive Brown set up a non-commercial organization, the Research Institute for Experimental Architecture, which is devoted to practical research and support for experimental architecture. Woods has lived and worked in New York since 1976.

PHOTOGRAPH CREDITS

*All photographs were provided by the architects'
offices, except in the following cases:*

Dorothy Alexander: fig. 8, p. 121

Farshid Assassi: fig. 8, p. 80

Rainer Blunck: fig. 3, p. 76

Tom Bonner, Washington, D. C.: Cover;
 fig. 1, p. 16; fig. 7, p. 22; fig. 13, p. 29;
 fig. 1, p. 72; fig. 5; p. 78; fig. 7, p. 79;
 fig. 10, p. 82; fig. 11, p. 83; fig. 13, p. 86

Dick Frank Studios: fig. 5, p. 41; figs. 6−8, p. 44;
 figs. 9, 11, 12, p. 45

Gaston: figs. 2, 3, p. 95; fig. 4, p. 96; figs. 5, 6,
 p. 97; figs. 7, 8, p. 98; fig. 9, p. 99;
 figs. 11−13, p. 102; figs. 14, 15, p. 103;
 fig. 16, p. 104; figs. 18, 19, p. 105

Jeff Goldberg/Esto: fig. 2, p. 38; fig. 3, p. 39;
 fig. 4, p. 40

Thom Mayne: fig. 2, p. 75

Peter McClennan: fig. 1, p. 106

Robert Morrow: fig. 4, p. 120; figs. 5, 6, p. 121

Grant Mudford: fig. 6, p. 78

Jean Nouvel, Emmanuel Cattani et associés:
 fig. 1, p. 90; fig. 10, p. 101

Daniel Oakley: fig. 10, p. 55

D. G. Olshavsky/Artog: fig. 1, p. 32

Paul Warchol: figs. 15, 16, p. 60

George Yu: fig. 14, p. 87

Gerald Zugmann, Vienna: fig. 2, p. 18; figs. 3−5,
 p. 19; figs. 8, 9, p. 25; fig. 10, p. 26, fig. 11,
 p. 27; fig. 12, p. 28; fig. 14, p. 31